DEATH IN VENICE

Making and Unmaking a Master

TWAYNE'S MASTERWORK SERIES

Robert Lecker, General Editor

DEATH IN VENICE

Making and Unmaking a Master

T. J. Reed

TWAYNE PUBLISHERS • NEW YORK
Maxwell Macmillan Canada • *Toronto*
Maxwell Macmillan International • *New York Oxford Singapore Sydney*

Twayne's Masterwork Studies No. 140

Death in Venice: Making and Unmaking a Master
T. J. Reed

Twayne Publishers   Maxwell Macmillan Canada, Inc.
Macmillan Publishing Company   1200 Eglinton Avenue East
866 Third Avenue   Suite 200
New York, New York 10022   Don Mills, Ontario M3C 3N1

Library of Congress Cataloging-in-Publication Data

Reed, T. J. (Terence James), 1937–
    Death in Venice : making and unmaking a master / T. J. Reed.
        p.   cm.—(Twayne's masterwork studies ; no. 140)
    Includes bibliographical references and index.
    ISBN 0-8057-8069-6 —ISBN 0-8057-8114-5 (pbk.)
    1. Mann, Thomas, 1975–1955. Tod in Venedig. I. Title. II. Series.
PT2625.A44T6455   1994
833'.912—dc20   94-4252
                                                              CIP

The paper used in this publication meets the minimum requirements of American National Standard for Information Sciences—Permanence of Paper for Printed Library Materials. ANSI Z3948–1984. ∞ ™

10 9 8 7 6 5 4 3 2 1 (hc)
10 9 8 7 6 5 4 3 2 1 (pb)

Printed in the United States of America

For Peter Ganz

Contents

Note on Translations and References   *ix*

Chronology: Thomas Mann's Life and Works   *xi*

LITERARY AND HISTORICAL CONTEXT

    1. A Culture and Its Pressures   3

    2. The Perils and Paradoxes of Art   10

    3. Reception   15

READING THE TEXT

    4. Unease and Omens   25

    5. Portrait of the Artist as an Older Man   33

    6. Destination, Destiny   41

    7. Idyll   51

    8. Alien God   59

EXTRA-TEXTUAL

    9. Connections, Genesis   73

    10. History, or What Dionysus Did Next   91

A Selection from Thomas Mann's Work Notes for

  Death in Venice   *103*

Notes and References   *113*

Bibliography   *123*

Index   *129*

Note on Translations and References

I quote Mann's novella in the Bantam Books translation by David Luke, referring both to it and to the other stories in that volume by simple page numbers in parentheses in my text. Of the three existing versions of *Death in Venice*, Luke's is the only one by a professional German scholar, and he corrects many literal errors in what was previously the sole copyrighted translation into English, by Helen Lowe-Porter. I have, however, sometimes made slight changes to the English, tacitly or expressly, so as to get closer to the effect of the original. The movement is always towards a more literal rendering of the German.

Other references have been kept to a minimum. Passages from works of Thomas Mann other than the stories in the Luke selection are located by volume (roman numeral) and page of the standard German collected edition. References are again given in parentheses in the text. For letters, I provide date and recipient only. All translations from works and letters are my own. The form *DüD* in the footnotes refers to the relevant volume of *Dichter über ihre Dichtungen*, a collection of the author's statements about his own work. For full details of all these sources, see the Bibliography.

Thomas Mann and his family in front of their country house at Tölz.

Photograph courtesy of the Thomas Mann Archive, Zurich.

Chronology: Thomas Mann's Life and Work

1875	Paul Thomas Mann born on 6 June as the second son of Johann Heinrich Mann, a leading businessman and senator of the north German Hansa city of Lübeck.
1892	On the death of Senator Mann, the family grain firm goes into liquidation. Thomas Mann and his brother Heinrich are left with sufficient means to live independently and try to establish themselves as writers.
1893	Leaves school and moves south to Munich, where his mother has settled.
1894	His first story, *Fallen*, is published in a Naturalist literary journal, *Society* (*Die Gesellschaft*).
1896–1898	Prolonged stay in Italy—Rome and Palestrina—with his brother Heinrich. Further short fiction appears in the leading literary journal of the day, the *New Review* (*Neue Rundschau*), published by the house of Samuel Fischer.
1897	At Fischer's invitation, begins work on a novel.
1898	Publishes his first volume of collected short fiction, *Little Herr Friedemann*.
1900	Completes the novel *Buddenbrooks* in May. Samuel Fischer, skeptical about the chances of such a massive work by a barely known author, suggests that Mann abridge it. The young author persuades him to publish it as it stands.
1901	*Buddenbrooks* appears, in two volumes, and is well received.
1902	Fischer brings out a single-volume cheap edition of *Buddenbrooks*. It becomes a best-seller, establishing Thomas Mann's fortunes and a broad popular reputation.
1903	The volume *Tristan* appears (six stories, including *Tonio Kröger*).

1905	Marries Katia Pringsheim, daughter of a wealthy Jewish academic family. Completes his only drama, *Fiorenza*, set in Renaissance Florence. Melodramatic and stylistically overelaborate, it never succeeds on the stage.
1905–1910	Works on a number of projects that are destined never to be completed: a novel on Munich society, "Maya"; a historical novel on Frederick the Great of Prussia; a major aesthetic essay, "Intellect and Art." Frustrated at his inability to make progress with them.
1909	Publishes the novel *Royal Highness*, on the surface a romance about a Ruritanian prince, but meant as an allegory of the artist's life. As the second novel from the author of the highly regarded *Buddenbrooks*, it is judged to be lightweight.
1910	Starts writing a further artist allegory, the story of the confidence trickster Felix Krull. Progress is difficult. Feels increasingly frustrated with his uncompleted projects and worried about how to repeat the success of *Buddenbrooks* with an unquestionable masterpiece.
1911	Vacation journey to the Adriatic island of Brioni in May. On 18 May, receives news of the death of the eminent composer Gustav Mahler, whom Mann had met the previous year. From 26 May to 2 June, stays on the Lido, Venice. Begins to write *Death in Venice*.
1912	*Death in Venice* completed in June. Published in the October and November numbers of the *New Review*.
1913	Begins work on *The Magic Mountain*, planned as a similar-length novella and comic pendant piece ("satyr-play") to *Death in Venice*.
1914	Outbreak of war. First essay in defense of Germany.
1915	Polemics continue, in particular against his brother Heinrich. In no mood for fiction, devotes himself to a long, brooding work of cultural-cum-political-cum-autobiographical reflections.
1918	*Considerations of an Unpolitical Man* appears just before World War I ends.
1918–1922	First reaction to Germany's military defeat is bitter withdrawal and a search for any remaining congenial forms of conservatism. Disturbed by increasing right-wing violence, resolves to make the best of the new sociopolitical situation. Public statement in defense of the new state in speech "Of German Republic." From then on, moves steadily towards social democracy.

Chronology

1924	Publishes *The Magic Mountain*. The intended novella has grown into a massive novel, taking issue allegorically with the social and political problems of the day.
1926–1933	Active as a member of the literary section of the Prussian Academy of Arts, where the cultural and ideological issues of the Weimar Republic are fought out by leading writers of left and right.
1929	Publishes *Mario and the Magician*, an allegorical tale of Italian fascism. Receives the Nobel Prize for Literature, but expressly for his first novel, *Buddenbrooks*. (The prize committee's most influential member disapproves of the liberalism implicit in *The Magic Mountain*.)
1933	Mann travels abroad in February, giving a lecture on Richard Wagner in various cities. Reports of the lecture are made the pretext for a hate campaign against him by Nazis and fellow-travelers. (Since the early thirties, he has been prominent as a defender of the Weimar Republic and an opponent of rising Nazism.) Mann's family warn him to stay abroad. It is the beginning of exile. After short stays in various places in France and Switzerland, settles in the autumn in Küsnacht near Zürich. *The Tales of Jakob*, the first volume of the four-part *Joseph and His Brethren*, is published in Germany, despite its Jewish subject.
1934	Makes first visit to the United States in May and June. Publishes the second volume of the tetralogy, *The Young Joseph*.
1936	Volume 3, *Joseph in Egypt*, appears. The Nazis deprive Mann of his German nationality. He takes Czech citizenship.
1938	Emigrates to the United States and holds a visiting professorship at Princeton.
1939	Publishes *Lotte in Weimar*, a novel about the older Goethe.
1940	Moves to Pacific Palisades, California.
1941	Becomes Germanic consultant to the Library of Congress.
1942–1945	Makes anti-Nazi broadcasts to Germany for the BBC.
1943	*Joseph the Provider* completes the Joseph tetralogy. Begins writing *Doctor Faustus*.
1944	Takes U.S. citizenship.
1947	*Doctor Faustus* published.
1949	Publishes *The Genesis of Doctor Faustus: Novel of a Novel*, which describes the roots of the work in the events of the time.

1950   Death of brother Heinrich.

1951   Publishes *The Holy Sinner*, a parodistic retelling of the medieval legend of Pope Gregory.

1952   Disturbed by McCarthyism and drawn to Europe for cultural reasons, but unwilling to return to Germany. Settles in Switzerland for his remaining years.

1954   Publishes *Confessions of the Confidence Trickster Felix Krull*, a completed first part of the novel begun in 1911 and abandoned in the twenties.

1955   Thomas Mann dies on 12 August in Zürich.

LITERARY AND HISTORICAL CONTEXT

1

A Culture and Its Pressures

The Germany Thomas Mann was born into in 1875 was just four years old. Until 1871 it had never existed as a unified state, and it had no coherent society of the kind England and France had long had. From the early Middle Ages down to the beginning of the nineteenth century, social and political realities for Germans were the local ones of the 300 territories, ranging from large principalities to independent cities, which made up the loose federal structure of the Holy Roman Empire of the German Nation. And when Germany did unite under Prussian leadership, it remained in some ways strongly regional and centrifugal. Political power might now be centralized in Bismarck's Berlin, but in places geographically or temperamentally remote from Berlin the old local ethos persisted: Mann's native Lübeck, for example, and Munich, the city to which he moved at the age of 18.

Culture too went on being divided as it always had been among the larger regional cities. Thomas Mann's move was taking him to an important artistic center, away from the cultural and economic backwater of Lübeck on the far north coast. His first novel, *Buddenbrooks*, seems at first sight dominated by the provincial reality he had left behind, a monument to a characteristic way of life. But the novel's immense success lay not in the local materials but in its precocious craftsmanship—the maturely unruffled style, the deft variations of technique and tempo that maintain narrative interest, the sovereign control of a long and complex history, the perfect balance struck between a relentless theme (*Decline of a Family* is the novel's subtitle), and the richness of figures and episodes that embody it. Mann was already, in his twenties, an accomplished European modern, nourished by the writing of Tolstoy and Turgenev, Flaubert, the Goncourt brothers, Maupassant and Bourget—and, above all, schooled in skeptical analysis by his reading of Nietzsche.

He was also a modern in his mode of work, rejecting emotion and inspiration in favor of discipline, detachment, and application. Like Flaubert, he scorned those who wrote easily (including, as his notebooks show, his novelist elder brother Heinrich) and labored over every sentence with ascetic devotion. This is the type of writer he makes Gustav von Aschenbach in *Death in Venice*, a dedicated and disciplined "moralist of achievement" (203). And as one of many strokes borrowed from his own experience, he locates Aschenbach in Munich. That background and the issues it focused for Thomas Mann are necessary factors in understanding the story.

If Mann would have been out of place staying in the provincial backwater of Lübeck, he was also out of place in Munich. Partly it was a matter of the southern city's all too easygoing character, which was at odds with Mann's sober north German ethos and moral sensibility, but partly also it was because of the domination of the visual arts in Munich, a city of painting and painters and models and artists' studios. Some of these artists, fashionable portrait painters especially, were established and celebrated, even ennobled with a "von" to their name.[1] But though they too must have been sufficiently "moralists of achievement" to work at their success, for Thomas Mann the very nature of visual art denied it the moral status of literature. Art could only represent the surface of things, whereas literature penetrated to the depths of experience. No literary mode had done this with more grim determination than late-nineteenth-century Naturalism, which was in its heyday when Mann began to write. His emphasis was to be different

4

from Zola's and Ibsen's and Gerhart Hauptmann's, less on the social, more on the psychological and pathological depths. He also felt less confident than the Naturalists did that reality had now been—or ever could be—exhaustively explored by science or sociology.[2] Nevertheless, they were analysts all, probing life in order to portray it. In comparison, the visual arts seemed to him positively misleading. By celebrating the beautiful surface of life and its beautiful successful people, they hid from view the abyss of human suffering which literature's "sacred torch" could illuminate. Mann treated that issue, and used the torch image, in the brilliant satirical short story *Gladius Dei*, set in a turn-of-the-century Munich "resplendent" with sunshine and art, on which the grotesque hero calls down divine punishment (73ff.). What for Mann was worse, Munich's love of art seemed to lead to a contempt for literature; though in gloomy moments he even felt, as a note for "Intellect and Art" says, that "enmity to literature" was "innate in Germans" at large.[3]

Society is not often in harmony with new departures in literature. Since the late eighteenth century, when the age of patronage in European culture ended, writers had increasingly felt alienated from bourgeois society by its "philistine" lack of imagination. Their criticisms and artistic provocations only alienated it in turn from them. In the Germany of Wilhelm II, the criticism of social ills was felt by a settled and complacent bourgeoisie to be itself a social ill. The kaiser himself, never slow to utter on any subject, said as much: the task of culture was the fostering of ideals. The critical portrayal of life was an unnecessary and ill-willed disturbance. Behind this façade of high principles lay ultimately a requirement of political conformity.

The gap between society and literature was widened by theories that art had its origins in biological decadence or even pathology. *Buddenbrooks* might seem to have bridged the gap by its success with a broad bourgeois readership. But while bourgeois readers enjoyed it for its richness as a family saga, its theme was precisely that the roots of art lay in decadence. It showed the "decline" of a merchant family which reaches its genealogical end point in the hypersensitive, musically gifted boy Hanno. He dies. But the real artist who shared his background, Thomas Mann, survives as a self-conscious outsider, cut off from the normality and competence of his Lübeck family background.

The story *Tonio Kröger*, however, soon made plain just how painfully Mann felt himself to be "not a human being but something strange, something alien, something different" (157), how powerful his fascination was with the contrasting "bliss of the commonplace" (161), how strong his impulse to achieve rapport with and recognition by the "fair-haired and blue-eyed, the bright children of life" (192), as Tonio Kröger idealizingly calls them.

Such recognition had been achieved by painters. Hence for Mann they belonged more to the realm of "Life" than to the realm of "the Spirit," where literature was located. But this meant that the visual art he rejected did also offer ways of adapting. To fulfill his social yearnings perhaps he only needed to turn away from the dark depths towards the beauties of the outside world, away from analysis to a more strongly plastic representation (an element which *Buddenbrooks*, after all, did not lack)? Since the turn of the century, critics who claimed to be more in touch with the needs of the majority than the avant-garde could ever be had been calling for an end to distasteful probings and for a new "healthy" emphasis. Young writers were able to make their mark by following this lead, as Mann thought he saw when he surveyed the literary scene. And if they succeeded by meeting the demand for healthy "regeneration," could an older writer with different tendencies still compete and keep his public? Mann saw himself in the situation of the old architect in Ibsen's play *The Master Builder*, whose work and status are threatened by a younger man. Looking at other leading writers of his own generation—Gerhart Hauptmann, Hugo von Hofmannsthal—Mann found they were perceptibly edging towards health and regeneration, "trying to get on the bandwagon," as he called it ("Intellect and Art," n. 103).

Mann's own response, which would shape Aschenbach's career too, was to conceive such change as a natural phase in a career. What was a writer's stock-in-trade in younger years (pathology, analysis) might give way naturally to something less radical and more easy on the public palate. But actually to plan such change seems dubious. In an essay, Mann talks about the Romantic poet Adelbert von Chamisso writing a "wild" youthful book and then "hastening to grow out of the chrysalis stage" and become a "master" (IX, 57). "Hastening to grow" seems a contradiction, a confusion of an act of will and a natural process. To "become a master" also in its way contradicts Mann's whole conception of the artist: the destined outsider becomes an insider. Yet it was something Mann consciously aspired to. It crops up more than once in letters to his brother Heinrich. It seems to have meant for him writing a new work that would match *Buddenbrooks* for scale and quality. He had done good things since that first novel—*Tonio Kröger* and *Tristan* of 1903, for example—but they were short, while his second full-length novel, *Royal Highness* of 1909, was found lightweight by comparison with its predecessor. Meantime, Mann's attempt to break into theater, the costume drama *Fiorenza*, had turned out, in his own words, a "fiasco" (letter to Heinrich Mann, 18 February 1905. He had plans enough, all for impressive subjects—a Munich social novel ("Maya"), a historical novel on Frederick the Great of Prussia, the essay on "Intellect and Art" that would summarize the cultural issues of his day. But time went by and nothing came of them: "One consumes oneself in plans and despairs of beginning" (letter to Heinrich Mann, 11 June 1906). Works that might have made him a pillar of the national culture remained jottings in a notebook. It was a decade in the doldrums.

Mann was also too honest not to have doubts about these ambitions. Did not the status of a master involve a settled complacency essentially untrue to art? He only needed to look at his brother. Heinrich had stayed independent of society. He was more inclined to criticize than to court it, and an alternative guidebook to the Munich scene declared him "proof against titles and all public distinctions." He was also plainly skeptical about the effects Thomas's "good" marriage would have on his writing. Thomas was aware of all this.[4] There are jottings in his notebooks where he insists to himself that he does not want to be a "national figure"[5]; for a time he plans a novella on how the old Goethe's dignity was undone (at 74 he fell in love with a girl of 17).[6] So at the conscious, self-critical level, the precarious nature of dignity is clear to him. And yet. . . .

7

This unstable pattern—of cultural change and challenge, of personal ambition and frustration, of inner uncertainty, uneasy conscience, and compositional problems—is the material from which Mann creates Gustav von Aschenbach. But he projects him safely beyond his own doubts and difficulties, as an older and fully established writer who has completed works Mann had not, "Maya," the Frederick novel, "Intellect and Art," and who, in order to get that far, has taken decisions Mann had not—yet. From being the kind of writer Mann had so far been, Aschenbach has turned himself into the kind of writer Mann was thinking of becoming. *Death in Venice* asks what consequences such a change would have. So, as Mann more than once implied (XII, 201, 517), the story is an experiment, one conducted by an author with the possibilities of his own career. And perhaps it also questions ultimately the very notion of "career," because, for all the hard work that is entailed by a "morality of achievement" like Aschenbach's, it is something different from the simple devotion to writing as such that marks certain pure spirits in the record of literature like Kafka and Emily Dickinson.

These issues were suddenly crystallized in story form by the events and figures of Mann's own journey to Venice in 1911: the strange foreigner at the North Cemetery in Munich, the sordid ship, the repellent dandy, the unlicensed gondolier, Tadzio and his family (the very boy has even, in his own old age, been traced), the failed attempt to leave the city, the cholera epidemic, the honest English travel clerk, the malicious street singer—"it was all given, it really only needed fitting in, and showed in the most astonishing way its capacity to be interpreted for compositional purposes" (XI, 124). In other words, inner and outer worlds came together for the writer.

The mixture proved nevertheless to have a will of its own. So far from allowing themselves to be freely disposed into a pattern, the materials (in Mann's later phrase) "precipitated" as a crystalline formation does and found their own form (XI, 123f.). It is, after all, the nature of true experiments that they do not allow their results to be prearranged, they are conducted with real, independent forces. Perhaps for that very reason Thomas Mann could feel, disturbingly yet exhilaratingly, that he was being borne along by the compositional process and its complexities rather than consciously guiding it. In more ways than one, the work surprised him. But then, as he reflected, that is what literature does for the writer. "Every work is a fragmentary actualisation of our essence and the only way we have of finding out what that essence is" (ibid.). *Death in Venice* was in this sense not so much given a tragic ending by the author; to be more exact, it found it. There are signs it could have been something quite other. The experiment worked itself out. In the process of being written, the story uncovered just who and what its author was.

2

The Perils and Paradoxes of Art

Death in Venice is the culmination of Mann's early series of "artist" stories. At first sight it seems to have the limited reference of what modern writers like Henry James, Rilke, Kafka, Broch, Joyce, and Hesse have virtually made into a subgenre; but the psychological course and tragic outcome of Mann's novella have a wider relevance. It treats love and death, passion and control, and the relation of creativity to morality. It lays bare the workings of the conscious and unconscious life and shows the complicity of character and will in the making of an individual's fate. It also embodies some striking paradoxes. It is an intensely private work couched in the tone of elevated public utterance, and it uses a style of polished formality to recount the breakdown of formative power. Its own power is the greater for pointing beyond the seemingly random anecdote of an erotic encounter in an exotic setting. It is also unintendedly part of a larger whole. The way an ordered existence and a carefully established mastery are overthrown by the "alien god" of deep impulse fits a pattern present in Mann's work from the early tale of a cripple's disastrous infatuation (*Little Herr Friedemann* of 1897), via the passion of Potiphar's wife for Joseph (*Joseph in Egypt* of 1936), to a final high point in the "hellish intoxication" of *Doctor Faustus* in the 1940s. In telling how a writer's self-discipline gives way to self-abandonment, *Death in Venice* already points all unknowingly to the roots of a larger catastrophe. For the forces of the "alien god" Dionysus are latent in the collective as well as the individual psyche. That is how Mann saw fascism from American exile in the thirties and forties, and that is why *Doctor Faustus*, written between 1943 and 1947 in an effort to understand the causes of the "German catastrophe," still has echoes of the Venetian novella. Taken together, this sequence of works is a profound contribution to human psychology and its archetypal portrayal.

To convey psychological insights that contribute to the dark larger picture, *Death in Venice* brilliantly combines two distinct kinds of narrative that would seem to clash: the realistic mode inherited from nineteenth-century fiction and the mythic mode which began to fascinate writers at the end of that age, when realism reached its limits. Mann's handling of myth in this his first systematic exploring of its potential can stand comparison with any other modern work. His layering of the mythic and the realistic modes is so deft that the movement between them is unobtrusive; the hints of something more-than-everyday are so rooted in everyday reality, and that reality is heightened with such delicate suggestiveness, that the narrative holds together as a unity. The writer who falls in love with a beautiful boy and dies of cholera is also the fated victim of a god, his vacation a necessary passage to death at an appointed place. In the real figures along his route, leading him on and mocking him as he goes, we fleetingly recognize mythic gods by their traditional attributes of physical form and costume. The Polish boy has his own mythic identity as Hermes, the guide of souls to the underworld. Venice itself is not just a random setting but an apt meeting place halfway between the traditional Indian origins of the god Dionysus and a Western culture that refuses to recognize him. Literature itself, as Aschenbach practices it, is part of that refusal: in mythic terms, he is devoted too exclusively to another, more placid god, Apollo. Overall, myth gives a resonance of universality to the novella's specific circumstances, and hence to the protagonist's tragic fall. There but for the grace of God goes anyone.

11

In another context, of course, the "specific circumstance" of Aschenbach's encounter and infatuation with Tadzio also makes *Death in Venice* a, if not the, classic narrative of homosexuality to set alongside those of Gide and Proust. Though sexual orientation is not itself the moral issue of what Mann later called his "moral fable" (VIII, 1069), no other motif could have brought together Mann's real experience and a handful of latent themes in such a compelling way. Certainly homosexual love was not, as has sometimes been claimed, the coolly taken decision of a writer at home in all forms of decadence who simply added this one more to his repertoire. It was intimately important for Mann himself and had been there for the observant eye before *Death in Venice* (for example, in *Tonio Kröger*). Mann's Venice experiences took him to the brink of new possibilities of public statement, before traits of personal and literary character and the social climate of the day combined to close off those possibilities and dictate the story's final shape.

Death in Venice also stands out among works of modern fiction by the radical doubt it casts on style and ultimately on the pretensions of art. It hardly seems so at first. From the very beginning it signals a style of its own in an unmissable manner. Every word is clearly being weighed, every phrase polished and placed for dignified effect. Readers sometimes find this excessive, some students are put off by it. They are in noteworthy company. D. H. Lawrence in his review of 1913 complained that the style lacked "the rhythm of a living thing" and that no sense of "unexpectedness" was allowed by its "carefully plotted and arranged developments."[1] Yet the style does not take the form it does merely to impress for its own sake. In the word Mann used when early critics said he had been presumptuous—that is, had used a grand manner to claim master status for himself—the style was "mimicry," that is, a means to evoke the world as a fastidious Aschenbach would see it.[2] This would make Lawrence's criticism a tribute to Mann's success, for the ring of the text had convinced him that the Thomas Mann of 1912 was declining into lifelessness at 53. But 53 is the fictional Aschenbach's age; the Mann who wrote the novella was 35.

On this view, the slightly too grandiose manner would be a conscious strategy. More, it would be the embodiment of a critical theme. (Moral for students: trust your impressions, at least long enough to ask what produced them.) For, once Aschenbach's dignified status has been destroyed by passion, it follows that the dignified style which was the artist's way of presenting himself to the public must itself have been a hollow façade. Aschenbach himself reflects not long before he dies that "the magisterial pose of our style is a lie and a farce," and that all the other pretensions of an accepted public figure are just as precarious: "Our fame and social position are an absurdity, the public's faith in us altogether ridiculous, the use of art to educate the nation and its youth is a reprehensible undertaking that should be forbidden by law" (261).

Yet this skepticism cannot be the last word—and not just because we should hardly be discussing Mann's work at all but for the continuing "use of art to educate." Even if the novella's style has elements of "mimicry," it is still the vehicle that carries the narrative at every point, even when the angle of vision is clearly not Aschenbach's. Moreover, the highly wrought character does fit Mann's own aspirations at the time he was writing the story. The descriptions of Tadzio especially could be seen as, at least in the first instance, Mann's own attempts at "plastic" form in response to the demands of his day, as well as being his response to a male beauty of which he was intensely appreciative. Nor can the sensuous writing that evokes Venice in its beauty and sordidness be only a rendering of Aschenbach's perception, since it conveys more than just his perspective; it is surely also Thomas Mann being graphic and sensuous in his own right, attempting something like the classicism to which Aschenbach had turned in his maturity. "A new classicism must come" (X, 843), Mann himself had written in 1911— written it there in Venice, on notepaper headed "Grand Hotel des Bains, Lido, Venise," in an essay which corresponds to that last "page and a half of exquisite prose" Aschenbach composes on the beach, with Tadzio in full view as his inspiration (236). "Mastery" and "classicism" were not just an achievement of Aschenbach's, constructed and coolly viewed by a detached narrator. And did not Mann himself, for all his doubts about art, go on to attain, as much as any writer in our century has done, the kind of fame and unquestioned public standing that he queries so radically in Aschenbach?[3]

So if skepticism undermines this novella, the reverse is also true. That is perhaps the most intriguing of its paradoxes.

3

Reception

OPINIONS

The most obviously striking features of *Death in Venice* are its homosexual subject and its highly wrought style. The story's reception has been shaped by the way critics have responded to these features and seen (or failed to see) their relation to each other. It has only become clear in recent years just how closely the two are linked.[1]

Mann was naturally uneasy about the effect his subject would have. As he waited for the first public reactions, he wondered whether he had not after all produced, in a phrase from the text, something "absurd and forbidden" (215). Attack came not just from the expected quarter. The poet Stefan George, who practiced his own neo-Grecian cult of a beautiful 16-year-old youth—the dead Maximilian Kronberger, celebrated as "Maximin"—declared that *Death in Venice* had "drawn the highest things down into the sphere of decay."[2] The leading homosexual propagandist of the day, Kurt Hiller, called the story "an example of moral narrowness" which was unexpected from the author of *Buddenbrooks*, and he accused Mann of putting love for a boy on a par with cholera.

Surprisingly, there was not the mass expression of moral outrage that might have been expected from the guardians of public decency. There were rejections of homosexuality, but no suggestion that Mann or his story was defending it. It was easy to assume that a specialist in decadence had found another decadent subject. The literary treatment seemed to confirm this. The novella's final form as what Mann was later to call a "moral fable," the devices that distance the narrator from his character, the elevated style and noble tone, which are themselves a form of detachment, and, of course, the tragic ending (one Catholic critic even suggested Aschenbach's death was a necessary punishment for his "sinful thoughts")—all these elements visibly put Mann on the "right" side.

The story's elevated style was seized on by friend and foe. Mann's archenemy Alfred Kerr touched a sore point with his sneer that Mann was always writing about "real writers" (*Dichter*) without being one himself. Linked with this was the other by now clichéd criticism that the text lacked "life" because its author could make no direct "naive" contact with life (Carl Busse)—an insight Mann had handed to critics on a plate by the confessions of *Tonio Kröger*. Writers like Mann and Flaubert, it was alleged, had to make a virtue of necessity and create what they could from a deficiency of "life," whereas "real" creativity like that of the Greeks or of Goethe sprang from a superfluity of life which flowed spontaneously into art. These criticisms hark back to the irrationalism of Nietzsche, for whom Flaubert was *the* example of modern creativity. They are echoed again in D. H. Lawrence's demand for a live organic style.[3]

Friendly voices too were declaring that the new work put its author in a class with Flaubert, the linkage now meant as praise for a stylistic tour de force. *Death in Venice*, it was argued, had turned psychology into high literary art and created an objective portrait from the analysis of a subjective condition. Both camps were taking the style at face value as its author's, the one in order to decry its lifelessness or pretensions, the other so as to praise its achievement. Neither thought to link the story's own style with its theme of the moral dubiousness of style itself.

In due course Mann himself proved able to forget the story's warning of what "classical" style and "mastery" might conceal. By 1918 an interviewer was telling him that the younger generation now preferred his traditional mode of writing to the wild innovations of the Expressionists, and that the key work in establishing a new German tradition was *Death in Venice* with its "remarkable atmosphere of classicity."[4] Mann accepted this with a good grace. The "new classicity," which in Venice he had declared "must come," apparently *had* come, and in the form after all of the Venice novella itself. His growing repute now made it possible to reclaim as his own the style he had distanced from himself as "mimicry."

It was less easy to reclaim the homosexual subject as equally his own. In the following decades, as Mann became an established international classic (which, of course, means more than having written works with outwardly "classical" qualities), the stylistic mastery of *Death in Venice* went on being emphasized. Arguably this was at least in part a displacement activity of critics that allowed them to pass over in silence the story's taboo subject, or at any rate not to probe the author's own relation to it. Mann gave scarcely a public hint of how close that relation was. Only when his letters began to be published did it become clear that there had at first been an affirmative and only after that a critical treatment of the theme.[5]

It remained for a more recent phase of criticism to read both this change of direction and its public aftermath, Mann's management of the reception process through his own authorial comments, as a failure of nerve. *Death in Venice* became "a provocation that was never understood" and that was made to seem "harmless" by the later statements of both author and commentators. And yet, when the critic asks, "What is left of an artist's boldness if he is not prepared to stand by it with his social persona?" the answer is not as simple as the rhetorical question implies.[6] It is easy now to ridicule *Death in Venice* for its "cultivated" treatment of a taboo theme, and to belittle Thomas Mann for timidity about his sexual orientation. But forthright confession and confrontation may not be the best literary tactic for changing the attitudes of society, as the case of Oscar Wilde shows. In contrast, the high formality and moral components of *Death in Venice* made it a difficult target to attack, and over the years this has had important consequences for the way its subject is viewed. Alfred Kerr's sarcastic comment that the novella had made "pederasty acceptable to the cultivated middle classes" has some truth in a more straightforward sense.

Old attitudes, of course, remained in force, and as late as the year before Mann died a letter from a German correspondent attacked *Death in Venice* as a "perverted" and "irresponsible" work. Mann replied by invoking the country he had just left against the continent he had returned to: "In America it is regarded as 'classical,' a sign surely that even and especially in that puritanical sphere it is not felt to be immoral." The story is indeed not immoral, he insists, because it is a "confession, the product of a thinking conscience and a pessimistic love of truth" (letter to Jürgen Ernestus, 17 June 1954). With notable patience—one wonders whether Aschenbach in his great days would have "performed the social . . . duties entailed by his reputation" (200) quite as conscientiously as this—the old writer tries once more to explain the familiar issues, down to that final querying of the public's trust in art and artists. But he now goes a step further: "In all this sceptical and suffering pessimism there is much truth, perhaps exaggeration of the truth and therefore only half-truth." In other words, revelations are not the final word, because the honest act of making them is part of the moral picture. So if *Death in Venice* "betrays the dignity of art and the artist," then his correspondent "might consider whether it is not through this conscientious betrayal that the artist's dignity is regained." And what Mann did not openly confess always lay just beneath the story's surface. It has become clear in later perspective.

ADAPTATIONS

Part of a work's reception is the way it is adapted in other media. In 1921 Thomas Mann was delighted by the portfolio of illustrations for

Death in Venice drawn by Wolfgang Born. Mann liked the shift away from the Naturalistic mode and from the story's more obvious "sensationalistic" motifs. Born had picked up the fleeting reference to Saint Sebastian (202) as an emblem for Aschenbach's work, and in the drawing entitled "Death" he had drawn Aschenbach with a startling likeness to Gustav Mahler, even though he could not know Mann had secretly used Mahler's features as a model for his description of Aschenbach (206). So language could after all communicate things seen, as visual art does.

More complex and challenging are the two major adaptations of more recent date and the critical questions they raise: Luchino Visconti's film, with Dirk Bogarde in the role of Aschenbach; and Benjamin Britten's opera, in which the Aschenbach role was created by Peter Pears. Whatever qualities each of these works has within its own art, they offer a stark contrast as adaptations, the one making radical changes, the other following as far as the medium allows the lines of the original.

Visconti's changes undo thematic links that hold Mann's novella together, and he adds motifs which further confuse the issue. His Aschenbach has been turned into a composer, perhaps on the mistaken assumption that Mann borrowed more from Mahler than his given name, facial features, and the public impact of his death. Making Aschenbach a musician breaks the story's causal connection between the protagonist's literary aesthetic and his passion for Tadzio. There is no equivalent in music for the change of emphasis in Aschenbach's career from critical insight to the appreciation of external beauty, or at any rate no attempt is made to provide one. And there is no possibility of showing that Aschenbach's art has been repressing Dionysus, since music is by its nature *the* Dionysian art. Another vital part of Mann's conception is removed when the composer's new work is hissed at a public performance, and when the invented figure of a friend, in an abstract discussion that bears no relation to anything in the novella, positively rants at him. This is plainly not a respected Aschenbach, much less a pillar of the national culture. But if there is no master status to undo, any revelation that makes art and the artist questionable loses most of its point. The story is reduced to the homosexual encounter, with a boy rather less innocent than Mann's Tadzio. Visconti adds a reference to a later Mann work (the boat that brings Aschenbach to Venice has the same name as the prostitute-love of the composer in *Doctor Faustus*); but this seems gratuitous and does not make up for the loss of motifs that do matter in the story he is adapting. We are left with the adagio from Mahler's Fifth Symphony haunting the background and the atmospheric beauty of Venice, which a camera can hardly miss. What the film does miss is the chance to do something the medium is ideally suited to, namely, portray the silent solitary figure, whose inner monologue could have been made up from the fragments of thought the text attributes to him.

Benjamin Britten's librettist tries to do something like this, but the operatic medium is less accommodating than film would have been.[7] It is hard for opera to thrive on silence, and from the first the libretto has to make Aschenbach in his isolation (there are no invented characters for him to talk to here) explicitly describe himself and analyze his problems. This would be awkward enough in any operatic situation, but it is especially so when part of the story's point is that the character fails to recognize what is going on inside him. Mann's subtle transitions from narrator voice to character, from suppressed or semiawareness to full realization, have to be made more abrupt in the opera. But against that, Britten and his librettist strive to be faithful to both the detail and the spirit of the original, as the composer always had been in his settings of literary works (Melville's *Billy Budd*, Crabbe's *Peter Grimes*, Shakespeare's *A Midsummer Night's Dream*, James's *The Turn of the Screw*, and Wilfred Owen's poetry in the *War Requiem*). Their one drastic innovation, turning Tadzio into the glorious victor in a balletic beach festival of athletics, mistakes his delicate beauty for superior robustness. Structurally, however, the parts composed for the competing voices of Apollo and Dionysus make the tragic point of the work and are true to the novella's deepest conception.

When they met years earlier, Thomas Mann apparently expressed a hope that the young Britten would make an opera of *Doctor Faustus*. It would have been a daunting task to compose even samples of the composer hero's extensive—and in part diabolically inspired—oeuvre. But short of that grandiose idea, Mann would have been well pleased that of all his works *Death in Venice* should be set by a composer close to it in spirit, whose own last work it was before he died.

READING THE TEXT

4

Unease and Omens

The opening chapter of *Death in Venice* does two contradictory things at once. It builds up the dignified world of an established writer and at the same time shows it beginning to crumble. We are drawn into taking Gustav von Aschenbach's status seriously—perhaps even a touch solemnly—yet we are also invited to have doubts.

All this is done in two ways: through direct statement and through the subtler suggestions of narrative style. That Aschenbach since his fiftieth birthday has enjoyed noble rank, and that he can "feel calmly confident" in the "mastery" which has "brought him national honour" (199)—this information is clear. But his prestige is also encoded in the kind of elevated phrases that describe his writing and his daily routine. His current work has reached "a difficult and dangerous point which demanded the utmost care and circumspection, the most insistent and precise effort of will" (195), a choice of words that makes the highest claims both for the importance of the task and for the standing of the craftsman. This is not any old writer, but one who has long been fulfilling the larger commissions of the European mind (198). Even so banal a thing as Aschenbach's afternoon rest seems almost ceremonial in the original German, where his "refreshing daily siesta" (195) is called, literally, an "unburdening slumber" (VIII, 444). Much the same is true of the terms in which, unobtrusively, Aschenbach's every perception and response to experience is evoked. There is a detached superiority in the way he "briefly surveyed" the scene of popular enjoyment at an open-air restaurant in the Englischer Garten (195) before continuing his dignified progress. Later, faced with two possible explanations for the sudden appearance of the out-landish stranger who sets the tragic course of events in motion, there is a fastidious detachment and dignified formality in the way Aschenbach, "without unduly pondering the question, inclined to the former hypothesis" (196). These are only the more prominent details in a prose of consistently high stylistic register. What it introduces us to is a personal world of intellectual achievement and control, of legit-imate authority, of public standing long and easily taken for granted. This is the mode of life of a master.

Like his positive pretensions, Aschenbach's problems too are conveyed in part by explicit statement and in part by less direct means. This distinction becomes more important than in the positive buildup, because the less direct means now come nearer to suggesting how grave the situation is and they suggest to us what is not clear to Aschenbach. Indeed, they mark the point where a crisis begins to work itself out. The explicit narrative statements only tell us what Aschenbach himself is aware of, what he is prepared to admit—that he is meeting with difficulties in his work on the current book; that he feels a "growing weariness which no one must be allowed to suspect nor his finished work betray by any telltale sign of debility or lassi-tude" (198); and that he even has a suspicion something may now be wrong with the whole spiritual economy which has made it possible for him to be so grandly productive in the past: "Was enslaved emo-tion now avenging itself by deserting him, by refusing from now on to bear up his art on its wings, by taking with it all his joy in words, all his appetite for the beauty of form?" (199).

To this extent Aschenbach is a worried man, but perhaps not yet more than that. Creative professional work like his *is* stressful in mod-ern times. One reason the public of the day has acclaimed him, we later learn, is that the characters in his novels embody precisely this contemporary truth. Through these figures he has spoken up for "all those who work on the brink of exhaustion" (203). His own art has always been hard work, a heroic struggle inspired by a "morality of achievement." So the difficulties he has met with when the story opens may be just one more phase in that struggle, a consequence of his years that may be mitigated, if not wholly overcome, by "not bending the bow too far," i.e., by simply taking a break. His decision to do that seems reassuringly rational; it is what results when a sudden violent impulse has been brought under the control, typically, of "common sense and self-discipline" (198).

The reader is not meant to assent to all this rational taming and tidying of Aschenbach's experience. For we have been made to feel how disturbing the experience was that brought on the travel impulse. The discrepancy between the violent power of the disturbance and Aschenbach's almost trivializing reaction is meant to tell its own story. Dramatic irony is already being established because we see deeper than the character does. Though much is done to draw us into his viewpoint—for example, the repeated "now" in the opening paragraph discreetly enlists our sympathy for this hard-driven writer whose work has "now reached a difficult and dangerous point," and whose afternoon repose is "now so necessary to him"—there are also clear hints of an alternative viewpoint, an alternative way both to understand what happens and, eventually, to judge it. This interplay between two viewpoints is a central feature of the story, and it is made possible by the subtle and pervasive modern technique known as "free indirect style" (in German, *erlebte Rede*). What at first sight seems to be narrator statement is often only the character's view, skillfully eavesdropped. Once we sense this, doubt undermines his—and our—certainties.[1]

But what does happen in this first chapter that is so overwhelming for Aschenbach? And why is his reaction inadequate? Waiting at a tram stop by the North Cemetery in Munich, he sees a stranger standing outside the mortuary chapel. Their eyes meet and Aschenbach is faced down, but he at once puts this from his mind. Only on the tram does he think of looking round for the man, but he is no longer anywhere to be seen, on board the tram or in the street. On the face of it, the incident is no more than slightly odd. The man's appearance, at least until he grimaces, is only "slightly unusual," a matter of some features of his dress and his non-Bavarian ethnic type, and the confrontation is only a minor embarrassment. At first sight, normality has not been much disturbed. Yet Aschenbach, immediately after their eyes meet, has a startlingly intense vision:

> Whether his imagination had been stirred by the stranger's itinerant appearance, or whether some other physical or psychological influence was at work, he now became conscious, to his complete surprise, of an extraordinary expansion of his inner self, a kind of roving restlessness, a youthful craving for far-off places, a feeling so new or at least so unaccustomed and forgotten that he stood as if rooted, with his hands clasped behind his back and his eyes to the ground, trying to ascertain the nature and purport of his emotion. (197)

The conclusion Aschenbach comes to is dismissive and reductive: what the vision sprang from was "simply a desire to travel" (197). The original German makes it plainer that this is Aschenbach's inner voice speaking, reassuring himself: "It was wanderlust, nothing more." The "was" may sound as if this has the narrator's authority; as often with free indirect style, there is no single feature of syntax or vocabulary that would link the utterance unambiguously with the character. Yet those "nows" in the opening paragraph already have begun to draw us into his viewpoint. Our hunch—and everything in the later course of the story will confirm it—is that the narrator's voice is infiltrating and presenting the character's view. "It is wanderlust, nothing more" is what Aschenbach says to himself, or thinks, or vaguely feels as one of those impressions that make up our consciousness for much of the time without necessarily being put into words. The narrator gives it clear formulation, but he also, by turning the character's "is" into the "was" of narrative, makes it into a fact of the fiction like any other. The diagnosis may not be true, but it is what the character feels in response to experience. Thought and feeling are no longer what they seemed in earlier fiction, coolly detached agencies, a sovereign self-consciousness standing to some extent above events and the more able to cope with them. They have become integrated into events, they *are* the crucial events. This change relates to free indirect style and its view of the world in general, but it is also quite specifically relevant to Aschenbach, whose thinking does not cope with events, indeed, in some respects has consciously given up the effort to do so. All this, free indirect style communicates with the lightest of touches.

What makes Aschenbach's explanation fall so pathetically short is the power of the vision, which even he immediately afterwards has to admit to himself. (It *is*, I think, still Aschenbach's thought we are hearing, for at least a further half-sentence, as he reflects on "the nature and purport of his emotion" and half goes back on his first, all-too-glib explanation.) For the words "It was wanderlust, nothing more" come at the start, not the end, of a paragraph; they are not a conclusion, they start an exploration. The text goes on after a semicolon, "but in the form of a veritable attack, intensified"—and what now follows renders Aschenbach's inner experience, again without implying that he verbalized it himself in this form—"intensified to the point of passion, of hallucination even. His desire became visionary, his imagination, which had not yet come to rest after the hours of work, conjured up an exemplary picture of all the wonders and terrors of the manifold earth, which it strove to embrace all at once; he saw, saw a landscape" (197). And what then unfolds is the picture of a tropical swamp, a water-wilderness of almost lewdly luxuriant plants and grotesque or threatening creatures ("the glinting eyes of a crouching tiger" [197]). The vision in all its detail is held together in a single long sentence, whose rhythmic force is sustained by the absence (in the original) of major punctuation rests, its visionary power renewed by the simple repetition of the dominant verb "saw." By omitting the pronoun "he" before these repetitions, the original conveys the intensity of Aschenbach's vision. Each (so to speak) unprefaced recurrence of the same verb is like a catching of his breath as a new wave of vision hits the involuntary watcher even before the last one has ebbed. The syntactic-stylistic effect is brought out by a comparison not just with the English translations, but with a weaker version of this paragraph in a 1912 bibliophile edition of the story.[2] No wonder that, from this visionary seeing, Aschenbach's "heart throbbed with terror and mysterious longing" (197). What he feels stirring is plainly a good deal more, after all, than just wanderlust.

But in what sense more? What can such an intense and exotic vision credibly be caused by, and what can it plausibly imply when it suddenly overcomes a staid twentieth-century character who has merely had a somewhat odd encounter? "His heart throbbed with terror and mysterious longing"—at a banal tram stop in a realistically described modern Munich. The story's opening pages are topographically precise and matter-of-fact, with their names of districts and streets and the Englischer Garten and the open-air restaurant. These are all places where Aschenbach is at home, and the kind of places where the modern reader, whether he happens to know Munich or not, in principle feels at home. Such everyday locations are certainly not as a rule the setting for intense visions and threatening epiphanies.

Yet despite the familiarity of setting, what we are told does nevertheless have a faintly alien feel. This is the edge of a populous city, but "as it happened . . . there was not a soul to be seen" in the vicinity of the tram stop, and "not one vehicle" passing along two main thoroughfares. That is not impossible, of course, any more than it is impossible to explain how the stranger was suddenly there, even if it is "not entirely clear" (196). Plausible explanations can similarly be found for his violent grimace (perhaps the sun was in his eyes, or perhaps he had a permanent facial deformity). And no doubt yet more explanations could be found for his equally sudden disappearance, though the chapter ends before Aschenbach can pursue them. But these circumstances, none of which strain credulity when taken singly, have a cumulative effect. Specifically, they make the stranger's appearance seem like a dramatic entrance staged just for Aschenbach. The theater, moreover, is one of death—a perfectly real chapel, of course, in the actual North Cemetery of Munich,[3] yet suddenly appropriated by this stranger with his bared teeth and his "air of imperious survey" for the purpose of a mysterious communication to his audience of one. It all creates "an extraordinary expansion" of Aschenbach's "inner self," and it opens a visionary window in his imagination, stirs unwonted emotions, and (as it turns out) fatefully alters the course of his life.

So although we are on the real streets of Munich in the year 19 . . and will shortly be on the equally real beaches and squares and canals of Venice, we are not quite at ease in either city. Indeed, we are less at ease from the outset than Aschenbach himself, who naturally enough soon regains his balance and sense of normality. We are seemingly located in modern reality and modern realism, but we are near the edge of such certainties as they offer. True, there has been nothing decisive to carry us into a different reality and a different literary mode, as there is in (say) the first sentence of Kafka's *Metamorphosis*, which pushes us decisively over the edge into the surreal by announcing that the protagonist awoke one day to find himself transformed into a beetle. Nor will there be anything that does so in the rest of the story; Thomas Mann will not—either here or, except very rarely, in his other works—abandon his footing in reality and realism. But already a touch of the uncanny has crept into Aschenbach's experience. That element, and with it our uncertainty and unease, will persist and grow. Together they will gradually suggest that there are more things in Munich and Venice than are dreamt of in Aschenbach's or in realism's philosophy.

All this, as already suggested, is a message to the reader rather than to Aschenbach. That remains largely true for the rest of the story: Aschenbach will only feel the disturbing effect of his experiences at the immediate level; he will notice the disturbing episodes and figures accumulate but will not see them as signs, much less glimpse the pattern they constitute. By the end of this first chapter, when they have only just begun, he seems fully settled again in his mind. Visionary terror and longing have begun to turn into a travel timetable; he has a plan to go south, though, as he reflects to himself, "not quite to where the tigers were" (199). That is the relaxed, almost complacent humor of a man who now feels sure of himself again. The remark will later rebound on him when, in a sense, the tigers come to meet him halfway. But for the present the force of his vision is already fading. By the time he begins his journey he seems to have forgotten it.

In this he is like other "sensible" Mann characters who experience vivid revelations or epiphanies that briefly lift them out of their real, and realistically presented, lives. In a late chapter (X, 5) of *Budden-brooks*, the weary and disillusioned Thomas Buddenbrook glimpses the ideal son who might have mastered life as he himself no longer can, and as his all-too-delicate real son never will. In a sudden compensating vision brought on by reading (and somewhat misunderstanding) the philosophy of Schopenhauer, he feels a mystical unity with all those human beings who have gone before him, especially those who had the strength and spontaneity he lacks. Something similar happens in *The Magic Mountain*. In its central chapter, "Snow," Hans Castorp skis out from his sanitarium, gets lost in a storm, drinks port, and in his befuddled state has a half-waking dream that embodies and resolves the social and existential issues that are daily argued out in the abstract, usually way above his head, by his two philosophic mentors, Settembrini and Naphta. Both these episodes contain an essential truth about the themes of their respective novels and about the situation each character is living out. The curtain briefly parts, and we share with the fictional figure a symbolic or allegorical message. After the revelation it closes again, and for realism's sake (it would not be plausible for his life to be transformed by it), the character forgets. The reader, of course, is meant not to. Similarly here, our remembrance of that swamp-labyrinth of "terror and mysterious longing," towards which the aggressive stranger has somehow pointed Aschenbach, remains a precondition for our understanding of everything that follows.

Indeed, placed this early in the action it is a kind of omen. There are further omens in these opening pages—the death's-head grimace of the stranger's distorted features; the cemetery chapel as the chosen setting for his entrance; the chapel's "Byzantine" structure and its apocalyptic beasts, tacit pointers to the Byzantine architecture of Venice and the city's emblem, the Lion of St. Mark. But these omens, which hint at what will finally happen and the place where it will happen, only confirm expectations that have already been raised in the reader by the story's title—of death, and of Venice. Aschenbach's vision, on the other hand, goes deeper than such externals as event and location. It hints at the reasons that lie behind his fate, or rather, more dynamically, at the forces stirring in him which his Venetian adventure will release.

5

Portrait of the Artist as an Older Man

Before Aschenbach can leave Munich, there is a fortnight's unavoidable delay during which he puts his personal and literary affairs in order. This routine matter is disposed of by the opening sentence of the third chapter, which flows on naturally from the close of the first. While we wait for that to happen and for the narrative proper to resume, we have the interpolated chapter 2 to read. It too tells a story, but not of external events. It recounts Aschenbach's career to date, reviewing the forms his literary work has taken and the issues and values his development embodies. It begins with the "works of his maturity," on which his reputation mainly rests, then treats his genetic origins, his fame and how he "manages" (200f.) it, his always delicate constitution, and the austere discipline he had to practice if he was to be productive. It discusses the special type of characters he created and their appeal to the contemporary public; the specific nature of his earlier work; his recent deliberate turn away from that literary mode; and the nature of his chosen new style (202ff.). It hints at possible dangers; seeks to justify a writer's becoming an established, even an establishment figure; and finally gives the few simple facts of Aschenbach's personal life and a sketch of his physical appearance (205f.).

All this is couched in a formal style that matches the high register of chapter 1. There we began to move in the world of a dignified major figure; now we are given the full justification of that status, that is, we learn what achievements have earned it. The narrative problem of how to make an artist-figure convincing *as* an artist is solved by a piece of mock literary biography. It may seem an easy way to give substance to a fictional figure, arbitrarily making up a distinguished career and inventing a set of impressive-sounding works. That would be so if the only thing needed were to equip the character with any old imagined past from which he could move forward into some equally arbitrary fictive future. But a fiction that is to express its writer[1] and persuade its readers must create its own necessities. Art is not, in a trivial, random sense, "free." Aschenbach's fictional "reality" is extrapolated backwards as well as forwards from the point at which we first meet him. Who he is must be consistent with how he acts. His past and the attitudes that have formed in him by the time the story starts are an important key to understanding its action and its ethical issues. Indeed, since he has enjoyed virtually no private "lived" life outside his creative career, apart from a brief happy marriage, what the text calls the "intensified life" of art becomes crucial. Aschenbach's temperament is traced back to a set of general causes, the mixture of austere Prussian and more "fiery" Bohemian blood. That is typical of Thomas Mann's conception of what makes artists. But beyond those preconditions, a very specific development has shaped the man who goes to Venice. We understand him not just as "*an* artist" but as "this particular artist" (not, as the Luke translation puts it, "this particular *kind* of artist").

Aschenbach's career is remarkable for two things. On the one hand there is the scope and nature of his work, on the other there is the way he has in recent years consciously shaped it. Roughly speaking, the first accounts for his standing, the second ultimately for his fall. The "works of his maturity" were calculated to meet all the demands an age might make on a major writer. He has treated a significant phase in German history in the massive novel about Frederick the Great. He has created a picture of contemporary society in the equally large-scale novel *Maya*. He has given a firm moral response to the aporias of modern relativism in the "powerful tale" entitled

A Miserable Wretch. And he has shown a command of the complex issues underlying the art of his day in the essay *Intellect and Art.* History, society, ethics, aesthetics; the greatest German monarch as a triumphantly handled subject; the greatest German aesthetic theorist (Schiller) as the obvious term of comparison—all this surely makes Aschenbach the complete literary master.[2]

And no less so because his achievement has cost great effort and discipline, more than anyone would guess from the outward appearance of "solid strength and stamina" (202) which his works present. That illusion is part of his triumph. His massive oeuvre has been built up with infinite pains from innumerable small inspirations. Aschenbach is a "moralist of achievement" (*Leistungsethiker*), an artistic exponent of the Protestant work ethic. For him, genius is not a matter of effortless superiority; everything great, he has somewhere written, is achieved against the grain, under pressure, "as a defiant 'Despite.'" He lives by that principle. It is typified by the early morning cold shower and the sacrificial religious devotion with which he "offers up" his morning hours to art. It is epitomized by the command "See it through!" (*Durchhalten*) which he has taken over from Frederick the Great as his own motto, and by the image a "subtle observer" has applied to the never-relaxed Aschenbach, that of a clenched fist which never relaxes. (The relaxing of Aschenbach's hands will mark the stages of his emotional adventure.)

Not surprisingly, the characters who people his books all have something of this same "heroism of weakness." The writer has projected his own mode of being into his fictions.[3] This fragile heroism constitutes, we learn, the "affinity" and "congruence" between him and his public that are in turn the deepest reasons for the acclaim his writing has won. So as well as a grand review of the named works that made Aschenbach's mature reputation, we get a second survey, this time of figures to which the public was drawn because of that affinity. They are figures not named, from works not named.[4] But the enigmatic hints of their fate and function suggest they are characters from earlier works; they do not obviously fit the plot of the "works of his maturity." Nevertheless, they belong alongside them in making the foundation of Aschenbach's eminence in the national culture.

Not so another aspect of Aschenbach's early work. Whereas he was able from the first to captivate bourgeois readers by his "palpably live literary representation, which had no intellectual axe to grind,"[5] at the same time he appealed to a less staid youthful readership by his "skepticism and irony," by being "problematic" and "radical," and by formulating "breath-taking cynicisms about the questionable nature of art and the artist." The key concepts of this practice were "knowledge" (*Wissen*) and, especially, "insight" or "analytical clarity" (*Erkenntnis*).[6] This is an aspect of his youth Aschenbach has since emphatically rejected, and the metaphors that evoke it imply that he was right to do so: "He had been in thrall to intellect, had exhausted the soil by excessive analysis and ground up the seed-corn of growth" (204). Intellect and analysis are here presented as contrary to nature: they tyrannize the free mind like an addiction, they consume resources that should be carefully husbanded for a productive future. So for Aschenbach to have put away these youthful things was a necessary part of that "ascent to dignity" which the text declares is the goal of every great talent (203).[7]

Even so, the way Aschenbach's resolve is narrated makes it sound like a paradox, even a provocation. It was, we are told, the "profound decision of the mature master to deny knowledge, to repudiate it, to pass over it with head held high, insofar as it was in the least degree calculated to paralyse, discourage or devalue the will, feeling, even passion" (204). The paradox and provocation lie in applying the metaphor of depth ("profound decision") to the rejection of all deeper understanding, and in labeling as "shallow by comparison" the original youthful impulse to take analysis as deep as it would go. It is, allegedly, "shallow" not to see that when analysis is thus pressed to the extreme it becomes a bottomless "abyss." Similarly, while we might think it was lax to reject the rigorous pursuit of knowledge, the text alleges on Aschenbach's behalf that in moral terms (paradox again) it is analysis itself that leads to laxity: "the laxity of the principle of compassion that to understand all is to forgive all"—Madame de Staël's famous aphorism "tout comprendre, c'est tout pardonner."[8]

The logic implied here can be put in a rhetorical question: when we know every last factor that lay behind, say, the behavior of a criminal, and if we accept that the criminal was indeed totally determined by these factors, how can there still be such a thing as moral blame? Psychology becomes an excuse to excuse everything. The notion of responsibility has been dissolved, and there is no ground left under our feet for moral judgment. In that sense, an abyss does indeed open beneath us. And as Tonio Kröger finds (153), for the writer who practices these things the abyss of knowledge and irony and skepticism into which he is constantly peering, if not himself actually falling, inevitably separates him from the society of ordinary people. Such unremitting analysis is also labeled (it may be implied that Aschenbach himself labeled it) the "indecent psychologism of the age." This is the dilemma Aschenbach has shown the way out of with his story *A Miserable Wretch*, where he has used forthright moral language to condemn vile actions (204). One imagines an almost Victorian voice thundering forth.

At the same time as Aschenbach came to believe that true "profundity" required a paradoxical return to a more "superficial," simpler view of morality, by coincidence (or is it, the text inquires, something more than coincidence?), his literary style suddenly took on a new "purity, simplicity, symmetry." These are all likewise "superficial" qualities, in the literal sense that they are aspects of the visible surface of things, undisturbed by analytical probing and benefiting from its absence. They are, moreover, qualities traditionally associated with the "classical" in art and literature, and the classical in turn is the category in which we expect to find many of the artists and writers who are by common agreement revered as "masters." It is therefore no surprise to find the two terms side by side in the sentence that summarizes Aschenbach's present position and aspirations as an artist: his mature works, we are told, had "an evident, indeed an intentional stamp of the Masterly and the Classical" (204). So the relation between art and knowledge, between analytical depth and unproblematic surface, is the issue on which at some point in his mature years Aschenbach's career has pivoted. We may guess that it was a central issue in his essay *Intellect and Art*, and we can perhaps assume that his argument resolved it—as is usual with artists who theorize—in a way that prepared and justified the shift in his own artistic commitment from "intellect" to "art."

So far, the narrator's rhetoric has suggested approval of Aschenbach's work and sympathy with his literary evolution—in simple terms, it has gone along with what must be the public's view of this great writer. But now, towards the end of the chapter, the rhetorical flow changes its course. In place of approval and sympathy, the narrator sounds notes of doubt. The authority of Aschenbach's new aesthetic, its adequacy as a response to experience, is questioned. Doubt begins with the word *intentional*. Can an intentional—literally, "a willed"—stamp of the classical and the masterly be wholly genuine? The word *stamp* already suggests something imposed from without. Should we be convinced by an appearance of classical mastery? Can the problems of art be truly resolved and the course of an individual artist's development be rightly settled by "decision" and imposition, rather than by a natural growth from within? Is it possible, is it legitimate, to *will* literary maturity?

The text poses rhetorical questions in this vein. It asks whether "moral resoluteness beyond knowledge and beyond subversive, inhibiting insight" (204f.) does not necessarily involve "a moral oversimplification of the world and of human psychology." This takes back the earlier paradoxical play with what is truly "profound" and what is "shallow" and comes closer to the commonsense view that neglecting or rejecting the knowledge and insight we have, or might acquire, can only be risky. This means that the moral achievement claimed for Aschenbach, the alleged "miracle of reborn naiveté" (204), may after all be merely a matter of sweeping uncomfortable questions under the carpet. It may involve turning a blind eye to too much. It is symptomatic that Aschenbach has excluded, as Louis XIV is said to have done, "every unrefined word" from his linguistic usage (205). How much of the world must that not involve excluding too?

And just as Aschenbach's moral (self-)simplification was also matched by a new attention to beauty of form in his work, so the doubts about his new morality are accompanied by doubts of the narrator's about formal beauty. Form may have a moral value because it is the product of the artist's disciplined work, and yet it may still be amoral, even immoral, as a finished product because the criteria to which it appeals do not necessarily have any substantive link with morality. Worse, beauty may even try to override moral values. The narrator, it seems, is still capable of the skeptical probing that has been renounced by his fictional colleague. Once again, as in chapter 1, he has first built up and then questioned something established, in this instance Aschenbach's thinking in aesthetics, together with the ethics that went with it.

But a brisk "Be that as it may!" has already anounced that we are breaking off the abstract argument and starting back towards the story track. The narrator stops only to defend Aschenbach's acceptance of public status, the outward forms of which were the conferring of the name-prefix *von* (Aschenbach "sensed the inner appropriateness of this honor" [205]) and the use of selected pages from his works as models of prose in school reading books. Finally we learn what little there is to know about Aschenbach's brief and now distant family life and are given a sketch of his outward appearance, for which the narrative borrows the features of Gustav Mahler, as it has already borrowed the composer's given name.

This detailed account of Aschenbach's career, interpolated into the narrative, shows Thomas Mann's need (and perhaps his sense of the reader's need too, in a dense and complex story) to have an explicit statement of the issues it embodies. In this it is like the lengthy discussion of an artist's problems in the central section of *Tonio Kröger* (153ff.), where that earlier writer-figure unburdens himself of his inner conflicts to his sympathetic painter friend Lizaveta Ivanovna. Or it is like the letter which Spinell writes to Klöterjahn in *Tristan* (122ff.), pouring out his hatred for the "unconscious type" of the bourgeois and declaring his mission to "analyze" it. All such abstract presentation, like the essayistic digressions found in much modern fiction, runs the risk of making the work of art seem overly schematic, and perhaps also of tapping off energies which the author might have used to shape the issues concretely. It needs, in other words, some aesthetic justifying. This particular example seems at first sight even more abstract than the discussion in *Tonio Kröger*, which is at least staged as a conversation-piece, with dialogue plausibly distributed between Tonio and Lizaveta in a real situation which has its own subtly suggested atmosphere. We are in the painter's studio, where Russian cigarettes and tea and sympathy are offered, a sunlit Munich is outside the north-facing windows, and there is "painter's fixative and the scent of spring" in the air (154), a disharmonious mixture which becomes for Tonio Kröger an emblem for the opposition between art and life they are discussing.

Yet the second chapter of *Death in Venice* does have its own situation and atmosphere too. It is not just an interruption in the narrative flow to provide information. As suggested above, it is "mock literary biography," a pastiche of what might be found in a standard reference work—a dictionary of national biography or an authoritative literary history. It has the ring of a measured public appraisal, and that inevitably gives a feeling of near-finality; for reviewing a life of achievement makes the great man's career seem nearly complete, especially when the fault lines in his work which will bring about that completion are highlighted. Altogether, it is like the obituary which journals of record keep ready, in need only of a last updating, for the day when the great public figure will die. To that extent the whole chapter is one more omen for the story that now resumes.

6

Destination, Destiny

What Aschenbach travels to find, as an escape from his literary impasse, is "something strange and random" (206). Yet apparently not quite random. There can still be right and wrong choices. His first stay, on an Adriatic island, is unsatisfactory. Aside from the particular annoyances of climate and clientele, he has an obscure sense of not yet having arrived at his proper destination. The German wording ("den Ort seiner Bestimmung") suggests a place he was "meant" to reach, without making clear whose is the intention. Suddenly he realizes where that must be, and acts. The account of this realization and his redeparture builds up to the final and culminating word of the paragraph: "Venice" (207).

This brings the narrative into line with its title, and in that sense Aschenbach is now on the right path. But "right" means that it will lead him to the other element decreed in the title, death. "Destination" is also destiny. It is his own instinct that has moved him in this fateful direction; throughout the story his actions do not just assent to a pattern of fate, they have a hand in creating it. But its reality *as* fate is also suggested, if not openly asserted—for to assert that ancient idea would sit oddly in a modern text. In this instance it is as if Aschenbach has subconsciously followed the symbolic pointers of chapter 1: the "Byzantine" mortuary chapel and the "two apocalyptic beasts" that hinted at Venetian style and the Lion of St. Mark. These were part of the weird encounter with that imperious stranger who dramatically embodies the external force of fate. To put it crudely (though this the text never does), "something" came for Aschenbach. There are further hints of an alien force that is concerned to keep him on his "chosen" path. The ship's purser sells him a ticket with a glib sales pitch, "almost as if he were anxious that the traveler might have second thoughts about his decision to go to Venice" (207f.). After serving Aschenbach, he calls for the next customer. There is none. As with the deserted Munich streets and the empty setting of the mortuary chapel, the stage is empty but for Aschenbach; it is as if things were set up solely for his benefit.

But decidedly not to his taste. The boat to Venice is not at all this dignified writer's usual scene. It is "ancient . . . dingy and black with soot," and everything on it is sordid—the "grubby hunch-backed seaman," the purser's "cavelike cabin" where Aschenbach's change is "dropped . . . on the stained tablecloth," the steward in a "grease-stained frock-coat," the "wretched meal," the captain who drinks all morning belowdecks with a group of loud apprentices (207ff.). Most sordid of all, in among these young men, and loud in his grotesque pretensions to be one of them, there is the hideous old fop, scrawny and wrinkled, with false teeth, but with rouged cheeks and garish clothes, mutton dressed as lamb (208). If voyaging to Venice is the "right" path, it is a dubious and disturbing one. "How was this possible?" Aschenbach asks himself. Tired and disorientated, he has "a feeling that something not quite usual was beginning to happen, that the world was undergoing a dreamlike alienation, becoming increasingly deranged and bizarre" (208f.). Not for the last time, he tries to get a grip on the situation: "Perhaps this process might be arrested if he were to cover his face for a little and then take a fresh look at things" (209). But at that moment "he had the sensation of being afloat": the ship has begun to move away from the quay. Just when he wanted to steady things, he is on an unsteady element—again, not for the last time. Venice is itself half water, "the yielding element" (212), and, in a phrase of Georg Simmel's, "the ambiguous city."[1]

Even arrival there turns out to be a mixed experience. There is irksome delay while waiting for the health and customs authorities (who, significantly for what happens later, only perform their duties "perfunctorily"); though there is also the "dazzling composition of fantastic architecture" seen when this "most improbable of cities" is approached from seaward (211). But any appreciation of beauty is disturbed by the old fop, now helplessly drunk, who importunes Aschenbach with "bleated" farewells and compliments to his "sweetheart." Repellently, he half loses his false teeth as he does so. Beauty mixed with sordidness is in the very grain of this novella. And a more specific pattern can be picked up here: when the "false youth" burbles out the foolish formality, "We commend ourselves to your kind remembrance," it is not just a meaningless request of his to Aschenbach, but a hint from narrator to reader. False youth and cosmetic rejuvenation are motifs that will recur, and the narrator needs our powers of "remembrance" to accomplish his ends.

Patterns and recurrence from now on are crucial. The narrative strategy consists in making us see them without making them too obvious. They are designed to structure the story's reality, but as with the notion of "fate," which they help to realize, they cannot be declared "real" by the criteria of realistic narrative. By the same token, they are not seen by Aschenbach, who inhabits the, to him, real world, even if it does sometimes seem disquietingly out of joint through the bizarre encounters of travel. Thus the unlicensed gondolier in his coffin-black gondola, who rows an unwilling Aschenbach all the way to the Lido instead of to the vaporetto station, is sinister enough in himself, with his refusal to obey his passenger and his grim words when asked about the fare, "You will pay"—without even, in the original German text, the polite address "signore" to soften them. But everything about him also echoes the earlier Munich encounter: the alien ethnic type (not a Bavarian in the Munich context, not an Italian here in Venice), the reddish hair, the straw hat, the prominent teeth. The two surely cannot (can they?) "be" the identical man. But the narrative does not say they are; there is no overt cross-reference to the earlier passage. Their similar features are not even described with the exactly identical wording that is found in the simpler forms of leitmotiv, and those similarities of feature are differently explained in the two passages: the Munich stranger's teeth were bared by a grimace as he looked into the sun (or was it a permanent deformation?), whereas the gondolier's are, naturally enough, bared by the effort of rowing. The explanations are entirely plausible. But they do not explain the uncanny likeness itself, once we have noticed it. If we have not (and the student at first reading may very well not—one student certainly remembers not noticing), then the explanations, with their own obtrusive uncertainties, are an extra way to *make* us notice it. In fact, a certain slowness to notice is arguably something the narrative strategy counts on: we are meant to feel the force of our attachment to reality and to realism, even as we feel the pull away from them. And the full literary effect then depends on our suggestibility to pattern, on our gradually more willing suspension (or at least half-suspension) of disbelief. We entertain the pattern these figures and their similarities make as a significant fiction, one that suggests an alternative reality that is not yet clearly comprehensible but is starting to be as strong as the "normal" one.

Significance, after all, commonly depends on patterns of repetition; conversely, any pattern of repetition begins to create meaning. A repeated scientific observation points to an underlying law, a repeated human action hints at a constant character, the repetition of a word or phrase underlines the coherence of an argument. From early in his career, Thomas Mann had used recurring motifs to create meanings beyond the randomness of mere fact, which was all that late Naturalism, the extreme form of nineteenth-century realism, set out to record. An appreciative early critic described Thomas Mann's literary method as "naturalism on the way to symbolism."[2] An obvious example is the way the outsider figures in his early work are linked from one story to another by a set of shared physical attributes, and their more robust opposites are linked by a different and equally consistent set. The reader takes in (or is taken in by) this schematic account of the way body and mind relate, and of the social consequences, while enjoying the narrative. The thesis behind the fiction is not quite met head-on, to be accepted or disagreed with. It takes an effort for the reader to stand back and ask what, beneath surface appearances, is the reality and necessity of things behind this allusive art. Is biological decline and spiritual refinement the reality behind the decline of the Buddenbrooks, as the novel gently and cumulatively persuades us? With *Death in Venice*, there will be an analogous question: just what is finally asserted as the reality behind Aschenbach's death?

For the present, there is a pause. Aschenbach is installed in his Lido hotel, and after the vicissitudes of travel resumes his status amid a discreet luxury that very much *is* his scene. The narrative can take stock of "the phenomena of his journey to this place," in a double sense, for his judgment can be read as a comment on the story's own balancing act and its likely effect on the reader: "Without presenting reason with difficulties, without even really offering food for thought, they were nevertheless fundamentally strange in nature, as it seemed to him, and disturbing no doubt through precisely this contradiction" (215). Once again, by denying that the events of Aschenbach's journey are even food for thought, the narrative makes them just that for any reader who has been insensitive enough so far *not* to find them unsettling. In fact, by now we should be alert to the probability that any word of reassurance means its opposite; we read it as part of a code of contrary suggestion. But a phase has been concluded. Aschenbach seems safe again in cocooning civilization, and this is emphasized by the note on which the paragraph ends. It evokes in appropriately formal language the sheltering refinements offered by a first-class international hotel. Aschenbach "gave the room-maid certain instructions for the enhancement of his comfort" and then "had himself conveyed . . . to the ground floor" (215). Disturbances have apparently been left behind him. The next encounter will be disturbing in a quite different way.

It is with the Polish boy Tadzio, who, insidiously, is one of the most refined products of this high-society civilization. That makes the encounter deceptively unthreatening. After the first shock of seeing "that the boy's beauty was perfect" (216), Aschenbach hastens to classify it safely with art, with "Greek sculpture of the noblest period," for example, the *Boy Extracting a Thorn*, and on the other hand links it with social privilege and family pampering (216f.). But there is a clue to the deep impression the boy's beauty has made. While he and his siblings wait for their mother, Aschenbach delays going in to dinner, "comfortably ensconced in his deep armchair, and incidentally [*übrigens*] with beauty there before his eyes" (217). Is his extra motive for lingering really so incidental? And if the boy, on his way in to dinner, turns and looks Aschenbach in the eyes, is it really just "for some reason or other" (218)? Or is the narrative's code of contraries again suggesting some deeper significance? True, beauty occupies Aschenbach's conscious mind over dinner, but it is in the (for an artist) perfectly natural form of abstract reflections on how it comes about. Reflection, appreciation, the pleasure of a connoisseur suddenly faced with an embodiment of the thing he most values, namely beauty—such detachment is the keynote of Aschenbach's responses. He seems secure and relaxed, his benevolence expressing itself through cultivated allusion and a touch of humor. He quotes a classical hexameter so as to cast Tadzio in the role of a latter-day Phaeacian (the Phaeacians are a relaxed, carefree people described in book 8 of Homer's *Odyssey*). In no time the narrative text itself drops into a matching hexameter rhythm: on Tadzio's collar "rested the bloom of the head in unsurpassable beauty" (220). Aschenbach's silent comment on the boy, "Good, good!" is a piece of "cool professional approval," as if of an artistic masterpiece.

His enjoyment, nature appreciated as art, is surely itself high civilization; the writer is in his element. It continues on the beach, where civilization as a whole is taking its ease "on the brink of the element," i.e., the sea. For the artist always struggling to achieve perfection, the sea is a competing if paradoxical perfection, total limitlessness in contrast to the firm limits of form. It offers a temptation to escape and rest which is already a kind of self-abandonment (221). It is also the background against which the boy's "truly godlike beauty" comes and goes, still kept psychologically at arm's length by a fund of cultivated comment. Thus when Tadzio is kissed by Jascha, Aschenbach again finds an apt quotation, this time from Xenophon's *Recollections of Socrates*. But both the action and, for all its easy humor, the Greek allusion start to touch on the theme of homosexual love, while the sounds of the boy's name, "ruling the beach" through the cries of his family, add a radically new excitement, they are "something at once sweet and wild." And when the boy emerges from the sea, perfect form from perfect formlessness, "the sight inspired mythic imaginings . . . of the origins of form and the birth of the gods." Aschenbach, for all his professional detachment, hears within himself the "beginnings of song" (223f.). Cool appreciation of statuesque form is mixed with the spirit of music.

But also with some confused and latently violent reactions: Aschenbach, the creator of literary beauty, feels "paternal favor" for the live being who "possesses beauty," but also a strange satisfaction that this delicate boy will "probably not grow old." There is an impulse to cherish, but also to destroy: something must be disturbing him deeply to evoke this response. And a third impulse makes itself felt between those two: the writer scans his mirror for the signs of age, "his gray hair, his weary sharp-featured face," then recalls all the achievements and distinctions he can think of. The anxious appraisal of what he has become in the flesh is followed almost desperately by a compensating appeal to what he has created in the spirit (224f.).

But all this passes without any sign that Aschenbach is clear about what is driving him. Once again, the stuff of the narrative is a not fully explained unease. Is that a factor in Aschenbach's physical malaise, which in turn makes him try to leave Venice? Or is it all just the oppressive sirocco weather? (*The Magic Mountain*, which was first designed as a sequel and "satyr-play" to *Death in Venice*, and perceptibly shadows its plot line in detail, will make a firm link between emotional, climatic, and bodily conditions; though it stays teasingly ambiguous about whether, in the high-Alpine atmosphere of Davos, love brings on illness or illness brings on love.) Is Aschenbach's malaise perhaps even a subconscious impulse to escape—it will prove to have been his last chance—from what he is not yet aware is his fate? It is true that climate is a factor he expressly recognizes; it is an old enemy that apparently routed him once before and made him cut short a visit to Venice. The sultriness, the sirocco, produce "simultaneous excitement and exhaustion" (225). His decision is immediate and rational; his will, which has been flaccid during the adventures and misadventures of travel and arrival, is firm enough now to arrange departure.

Yet something undermines his firmness. A new morning with hints of a change in the weather already makes him regret his decision. But it is not the only thing that leads him to delay and delay leaving, despite the urgings of the hotel staff. "It was indeed getting very late by the time he rose. It so happened that at that same moment Tadzio entered through the glass door" (227). But this is not a story in which *any*thing just "so happens." Using the casual to suggest the causal is another feature of the code of contraries, which by now the reader should be reading with ease. Aschenbach's sotto voce farewell to the boy is the key to this part of the text. Can any reader of the next few pages, which describe the botched departure, seriously believe that "what he found so hard to bear, what was indeed at times quite unendurable, was *evidently* the thought that he would never see Venice again, that this was a parting for ever" (228; italics mine)? It would have been more "evidently" so without that word, which we take at our peril for a firm statement by an omniscient narrator. After our accumulated practice, we can now only read the explanation as once more couched in free indirect style, and therefore as a façade behind which Aschenbach conceals the truth from himself, though not from a narrator who is only feigning nescience. His regrets at the prospect of never again seeing Venice thinly overlay his real regrets at leaving Tadzio. That deeper reality duly shows in the language: Venice is a "beloved city," and Aschenbach is a failed lover, no longer prepared (as he was the night before) to admit his own physical inadequacy and draw the consequences.

The botched departure is a classic piece of narrative even in this virtuoso text. There are sad images and rhythms for the "voyage of sorrow" to the station; then a quick sequence of confusion and delight in the scene on the platform (made more immediate in the original by a shift to the present tense, which the English translations do not try to render); and then the sprightly rhythms of the return to the Lido, with "the rapid little boat, spray before its bows, tacking to and fro between gondolas and vaporetti," the very embodiment of joyful release. Aschenbach is as happy as a "truant schoolboy." The literal German sense—an "escaped" schoolboy—sets off an even more ironic sequence. For what Aschenbach has escaped from is his attempted escape from Venice. The irony is that for the first time he himself now sees things as the work of a higher agency, but a wholly benevolent one. So he can relish "returning to places from which one had just taken leave, turned round by fate," and correcting a "grievous mistake." He can be secretly delighted by the incompetence that ought by rights to have infuriated him. He can welcome what is outwardly a "stroke of misfortune," a "visitation" (229). He can inwardly laugh at the commiserations of the hotel staff: "Pas de chance, monsieur" ("Bad luck, sir"), says the lift attendant. But there is, of course, a double irony that reverses Aschenbach's own reversals. He is indeed a "fugitive" (230), now recaptured and returning to a new room. The lift attendant's innocent words can even be read as true, as a darker frame outside Aschenbach's glee, giving their true ominous sense to the accidents that have brought him back.

So Aschenbach's first recognition of a destiny underlying his adventures is both right and wrong, both clarity and illusion: he is right about the coherence, but wrong about its ultimate direction. The mistake draws him willingly on towards his fate.

On one thing, however, he attains a clarity without illusion. Reinstalled, relaxed after the excitement, and musing with disapproval on his own "irresolution, his ignorance of his own wishes," he sees from his high window Tadzio coming back from the beach. Aschenbach shapes a jaunty phrase of mental greeting but feels it "die on his lips," feels "the enthusiasm of his blood," and knows the true reason departure felt so desolating, "that it was because of Tadzio" (230). This, then, is the "late adventure of the emotions" that he half anticipated as the boat lay off Venice (210)—its origins lie that far back, though Aschenbach does not make the connection. But his visible response points much farther back still, to the needs of a toiler in the spirit who had "'only ever lived like *this*'—and the speaker clenched the fingers of his left hand tightly into a fist—'and never like *this*'—and he let his open hand hang comfortably down from the arm of the chair" (201). Aschenbach has sacrificed physical and emotional life over years of intense creativity. That disciplined will has asserted itself only with difficulty, and then flagged altogether, when challenged by the bizarre figures and events of the journey. Now he willingly gives up the struggle with an emblematic "opening and outspreading of the arms," a "gesture of ready welcome and calm acceptance" (230). It is the first time since the world started to be out of joint that Aschenbach, the devotee of beautiful surfaces who long ago gave up the indecencies of psychological analysis, has looked deeply into himself. But it is too late now to make a difference.

7

Idyll

What follows is a fatal happiness, but happiness nonetheless. After his failed departure, Aschenbach puts off all thought of leaving Venice and settles in for a season. The weather seems to confirm the rightness of what has happened: the opening of the new chapter is all heat and light—the burning sun, the radiance on the sea, the glowing sand. Aschenbach idles as it was never in his nature to do before. Away from his strict routines as a "moralist of achievement" at his summer house in the mountains, there is all the time in the world to do so. "This place bewitched him, relaxed his will, gave him happiness" (231). He savors this ideal existence by recalling some lines of Homer's—Greek allusions will come thick and fast from now on—about the "Elysian land . . . where lightest of living is granted to mortals" (232; *Odyssey*, book 4, ll. 563ff.). He is consciously living an idyll.

At its center is of course the chance to observe Tadzio "almost constantly" (232). The narrator lingers over those observations as lovingly as his protagonist does, and to more literary effect. Like Aschenbach, he soon knows "every line and pose of that noble, so freely displayed body" (233), but unlike his character, he captures them in language. For Aschenbach, the boy is "more beautiful than words can express"; he concludes that language "can only praise sensuous beauty, but not reproduce it" (240). But the disclaimer makes us aware—and is probably meant to—how much Thomas Mann has managed to do just that. It is one of the ironies of free indirect style that the narrator can find words for the passionate perceptions of his character and take credit for formulating what his character despairs of saying—even while the narrative suggests it was fully present to Aschenbach's mind and on the very tip of his tongue.

These set-piece descriptions are aesthetic in a complex sense. First, Thomas Mann sets out to create verbal equivalents of plastic art—that was a conscious ambition at the time he wrote the story, and specifically to celebrate the boy was its first inspiration (see below, p. 83f.). Secondly, a last remnant of aesthetic disguise still conceals Aschenbach's true feelings. Though he has now realized that the pain of departure was caused by leaving Tadzio, and though he gives himself up unreservedly to the pleasures of the beach, still he sees the boy in artistic terms: in motion or at rest, running, standing, or lying, poised or posed, with his "finely chiseled arm" (233) and his "marble-pale skin" which the sun seems never to burn, Tadzio is like an animated statue. Watching him can be called "contemplation and study" (232)—the delight it gives is of a cultivated, aesthetic kind. Admittedly, its sensuousness has moved it away from Kant's austere aesthetic principle of "disinterested pleasure" and towards the one Nietzsche borrowed from Stendhal, that "beauty is a promise of happiness." Even so, it is enough to hold off for a while Aschenbach's final frank avowal of his passion. And this last, in every sense formal resistance appears strengthened when Aschenbach draws a parallel between Tadzio and his own literary aesthetic, between the beauty of the boy's living form and the "slender form" that he the writer, "filled with sober passion," labors to "set free from the marble mass of language" (234). But the parallel reminds us that the concern with beauty, a new devotion to surfaces rather than depths, was the chosen aesthetic path of the mature, deliberately classical Aschenbach, and is what has made him extra responsive—ultimately, that is, susceptible—to Tadzio. Beauty of form is an obvious link between them, but the analogy is deceptive: the beauty the writer creates is an end product of his "sober passion"; live human beauty may be the start of an anything but sober one.

Just as clear is what links Aschenbach's present state of mind and feeling with the aesthetic path *not* chosen, that is, with the "immature" values of his early work which he consciously discarded. This is made quite explicit by the narrative. In another minidrama of confusion akin to the failed departure from Venice, he tries to establish a "normal" relationship with Tadzio by speaking a few casual words. Failure again results. When he catches up with the boy, "a strangled and trembling voice" is all he could have managed, "he felt his heart, perhaps partly because he had been walking so fast, hammering wildly inside him" (237). The words "perhaps partly" are a façade-explanation of the kind the story has made us used to. At all events, it is now "too late" to achieve his aim. That is Aschenbach's view ("he thought at that moment"), and it is still perhaps Aschenbach thinking—though with free indirect style it is hard to be sure—in what follows: "But was it too late? This step he had failed to take would very possibly have led to . . . a wholesome sobering." In the next sentence, however, the "dual voice" has certainly split, and it is the narrator we hear critically recognizing that it really is too late and that "wholesome sobering" has been consciously refused: "The aging lover no longer wished to return to sobriety . . . the intoxication was too precious to him." The explanation of why this is so echoes what chapter 2 told us about Aschenbach's mature development: "Aschenbach was no longer disposed to self-criticism; taste, the intellectual mold of his years, self-respect, maturity and late simplicity all disinclined him to analyze his motives and decide whether what had prevented him from carrying out his intention had been a prompting of conscience or a disreputable weakness" (237). Aschenbach's "profound decision" to give up probing into motives ("indecent psychologism") has become a "late simplicity" that now determines his actions and omissions. The "too late" of this particular incident is part of a more general and necessary "too late."

Earlier warnings are being fulfilled. But some of Aschenbach's own reflections take us on to quite new ground. The form he strives to "set free from the marble mass of language" is described as "a model and mirror of intellectual beauty" (234). These words excite him because they suddenly suggest a yet more elevated way of seeing Tadzio's beauty: this too is a "model and mirror" of something higher, beyond the individual's bodily being. Looking at Tadzio, Aschenbach can feel he is "gazing on Beauty itself, on Form as a divine thought, on the one and pure perfection which dwells in the spirit and of which a human likeness had here been lightly and graciously set up for him to worship" (234).

This is not a notion from early-twentieth-century Venice, or Germany, but from ancient Greece. It is more, however, than the kind of decorative allusion that comes readily to the cultivated traveler, like the "Elysian idyll" evoked at the start of the chapter or the various decorative myths that will occur later (239). This one goes deeper, putting Aschenbach's devotion to Tadzio in a new and potentially ennobling context. It begins when he imagines Socrates in conversation with a young Athenian, Phaedrus, outide the walls of the city, and remembers the doctrines Plato put forward in the dialogue called by the young man's name. Plato's philosophical dialogues, the *Phaedrus* and the *Symposium*, give beauty a special place as the only meeting point between the realm of absolute values (the "Ideas" or ultimate forms) and human sensuous experience. All other absolutes of that transcendent realm—which, according to Plato's metaphysics, human beings knew before they were born but necessarily forgot when they entered on earthly existence—are abstract and beyond direct experiencing. Only beauty can appear, visible and tangible, before our eyes. When it does, we undergo a shock of recognition as we remember (for Plato, all education and initiation is a process of remembering) the higher realm we once knew. Since that is where all reality resides, beauty itself cannot be seized or possessed. But it can be known more directly than any other of the ultimate forms, provided that, even while the individual beautiful object or person is being loved, the lover looks beyond them and pays homage to the reality from which their shape is borrowed. The true lover loves intensely, but always symbolically.

Strange though this subtle doctrine may seem to a materialistic age,[1] it can be understood at least at a simple level by asking whether the lover of a beautiful person or the owner of a beautiful work of art could ever be said to *possess* the actual beauty of person or work. For the quality of beauty exists in a different dimension from the living being or material object that manifests it, whether or not we choose to think of this other dimension in Plato's manner as an actual realm of transcendent reality. Beauty is an appearance, a form, a relationship between physical elements, an intangible essence of tangible bodies which may consequently generate in us a distinct way of seeing and responding—distinct, that is, from the normal impulses of desire, acquisition, or use. Eighteenth-century German philosophy coined the term "aesthetic" to capture this experience. To that extent Plato is the father of modern aesthetics—even though his insistence that the reality of beauty (as of all other phenomena) lies in a transcendent realm is at odds with the concreteness and earthliness of art. This will be a crucial point at the novella's end.

But meantime, what *should* the human response to beauty be, if not straightforward physical enjoyment and complacent possession? Plato's answer is: a spiritual activity that will measure up to the high, indeed quasi-religious source of inspiration. For him, physical love and procreation flatly did not. Christian Europe was later to idealize relations between the sexes, but for the Greeks they had no romantic aura. Love between men did. It seemed (a logically somewhat shaky argument) to have more spiritual potential precisely because it lacked a biological function. The *Phaedrus* talks of "spiritual begetting" as something analogous to, but higher than, the production of physical offspring. Homosexual love might lead men to write poetry, to pursue philosophy, or to act bravely in a common cause. They might be inspired to emulation, to creation, to reflection, they might die together (some celebrated pairs of young men did) in opposing tyranny or defending their homeland. That these things were possible did not of course make them always actual. It was equally possible for a lover to fall short of the ideal, not reach beyond gratification, fail to see what higher reality was signaled in the beloved. This meant that the lover's response to beauty would be a judgment on the lover. Aschenbach, who is consciously savoring and quoting to himself what he remembers of the *Phaedrus* dialogue (235), duly recalls Plato's warning against "the lusts of the profane and base who cannot turn their eyes to Beauty when they behold its image and are not capable of reverence" (235).

How does his own case stand? Positively, it would seem. His mind is certainly clear about the issues, and "at this point of [his] crisis and visitation"—the terms make it clear that this is an important turning point—he goes back to his art (236). Not by directly describing Tadzio, but by working with the boy in sight, so that he can "let his style follow the lineaments of this body which he saw as divine" (236). The boy's beauty is the writer's inspiration, and he is mindful of its transcendent source. This meets the demands of Plato's ideal, and the text duly echoes words from the *Phaedrus* on spiritual begetting: "How strange those hours were! How strangely exhausting that labor! How mysterious this act of intercourse and begetting between a mind and a body!" (236).

If more is needed to make this appear a wholly positive turn, there is the way it relates to the problems that set the story going. Aschenbach's act of writing achieves—ecstatically—what the Venetian journey was meant to achieve in a more humdrum way, as a simple break from his frustrating labors: namely, the return of his creative powers and an end to the problem of writer's block that first sent him out for that afternoon walk back in Munich. His pleasure in writing again, and writing well, is correspondingly acute. Thought and feeling interpenetrate, and "never had he felt the joy of the word more sweetly, never had he known so clearly that Eros dwells in language" (235f.). To the happiness of carefree days in the sun is added the happiness of a restored creativity. It seems the writer's situation is doubly idyllic.

So it comes as a surprise, if not a shock, to find that the "mysterious . . . act of intercourse and begetting between a mind and a body" is finally presented in a negative light. For as Aschenbach finishes his "page and a half of exquisite prose . . . with its limpid nobility and vibrant controlled passion," we get a jaundiced comment from the narrator: "It is as well that the world knows only a fine piece of work and not also its origins, the conditions under which it came into being," for such knowledge "would often confuse readers and shock them." More negative still, as Aschenbach puts his work away, "he felt worn out, even broken, and it felt as if his conscience were accusing him as if after some act of debauchery" (236).

It is hard to see how Aschenbach has fallen short, at least in intention. Yet there has been an earlier clue that Platonic spirituality will be hard for him to achieve. No sooner had he entertained the thought of Tadzio as "model and mirror . . . of Beauty itself" than the narrator commented (more emphatically in the original than in the translation): "That was intoxication; and unhesitatingly, avidly even, the aging writer bade it welcome" (234). And if this warning note was sounded as a lead-in to the "Platonic" phase, what follows immediately after that phase is the incident where Aschenbach fails to establish a normal contact with Tadzio—which is presented not simply as a failure, but as a positive preference for intoxication, a refusal to be sobered. It begins to look as if the writer's consuming emotion for the boy can no more transform itself into pure Platonism than it could earlier pretend to be pure aesthetic contemplation. There is thus no way of escape for Aschenbach in the spirit, any more than there was in the body when he tried to leave Venice. He is in the grip of some larger, still unidentified force.

Towards the end of the chapter, Aschenbach, unsobered and in a heightened "poetic" state, draws on yet more classical allusion, or the narrator does so on his behalf: the beauty of dawn over the sea is rendered in figures of Greek myth as he muses on Tadzio (238). And in what is now unambiguously Aschenbach's own vision, the boy is transformed into the youth Hyacinthus, who died a tragic death because two gods both jealously loved him. Here the mythic "fine writing" becomes cloyingly sentimental and overdone. But it is fairly clearly the character's excess, not the narrator's, for the latter's cool, detached voice returns on the same page to make a psychological generalization from Aschenbach's relation to Tadzio: "For one human being loves and honors another as long as he is not in a position to judge him, and longing is the product of deficient knowledge" (239). A familiar word has returned, *Erkenntnis*, the analytic knowledge which the young Aschenbach pursued to excess but which his later self forswore altogether as something too subversive for literary decency (203f.). The suggestion is plain: it would have helped him here.

With no ordinary relations initiated between them, Aschenbach and Tadzio live in a tense mutual awareness. For the boy could hardly not notice such persistent attention, and he begins to respond to it, passing closer than necessary to his admirer's place on the sands, as if drawn by the magnet of powerful feeling. The unspeaking relation between them is in its way controlled and formal. But the formality is precarious, and a sudden encounter is all it takes to let that powerful feeling break through and declare itself fully. They meet unexpectedly, and Tadzio smiles at his admirer from close range: "It was the smile of Narcissus as he bows his head over the mirroring water, that profound, fascinated, protracted smile with which he reaches out his arms towards the reflection of his own beauty" (241). Again the image of the mirror, but now in a very different sense. It is no longer Tadzio who is the mirror, certainly not the "model and mirror" of absolute beauty into which Aschenbach's Platonic reminiscing has idealized him. Nor is he even the boy of the mythic simile who innocently fell in love with his own image. Rather his is the knowing smile of one who senses the power of his beauty over others, consciously enjoys both the power and the beauty, and uses his admirer—Aschenbach is now the mirror—to reflect his beauty back to him. Tadzio's knowingness is as far from the Platonic ideal as Aschenbach himself seems fated to remain.

For the last paragraph of the chapter shows the writer in desperate disarray. His composure is shattered by the "fateful gift" of that smile, he struggles to find adequate expression of his moral outrage at it. Yet moral outrage is hardly relevant, since beauty of form, as we were long ago warned, need not have any connection with morality, and may totally override it (205). So it proves. The openness of this first ever avowed communication between them drives Aschenbach into the open. In a posture not of relaxed acceptance, as at the close of chapter 3, but of overwhelmed physical helplessness, he utters in the climactic last lines of this chapter the inner truth he has repressed for so long.

8

Alien God

In the fifth act of a tragedy, events take an ever clearer direction and move with growing speed down an incline of inevitability. When the catastrophe comes, it may bring with it an understanding of its own causes, and even an insight into some profound principle—for the character, that is. If he achieves this most sophisticated form of what Aristotle called *anagnorisis* (recognition), then the gap of dramatic irony that has all along separated the protagonist from the onlookers or readers is at least partly closed. The tragic victim is thereby restored in some measure to the larger community, even if it is only for a brief moment before being finally destroyed. So there is a paradoxical double movement in these closing stages: deeper into tragedy, but as a way—the only way left, and also the price—of rising above tragedy. All these possibilities are fulfilled in *Death in Venice*.

The act of avowing his love has removed most of Aschenbach's scruples. Where once he relied on chance encounters, he now positively pursues Tadzio—on foot through the streets, with the disturbing possibility that their intricate twists and turns may at any moment bring him embarrassingly face to face with the family; and more melodramatically on the canals, half thrilled and half ashamed at the "roguish compliance" (244) with which he is served by a gondolier to whom this kind of intrigue is routine. And that is only part of the changed relation to Tadzio. The boy is now far from being an aesthetic phenomenon, the object of "devotion and study" as envisaged in the Platonic ideal. He has become the "idol" of a lover driven by "mad compulsion"—the original German echoes the Greek word *mania*, meaning a condition in which alien forces have overwhelmed and taken possession of the conscious mind. The emphasis has shifted markedly away from beauty.

That also applies to the treatment of Venice. After the idyll on the Lido, the city now comes into view more and more as the scene of the pursuit and is itself morally dubious to match the foreground action. From the start Venice has been a disorienting mixture: it is land surrounded, infiltrated, even threatened by water. Water is the "element" on whose brink "civilisation" is so precariously perched (220). It is "the yielding element" on which Aschenbach's weakening will was first shown up in the episode of the unlicensed gondolier (212); even further back, at the start of his sea journey to Venice, the "sensation of being afloat" made him feel "an irrational alarm" and disoriented him further as he strove to get a grip on increasingly bizarre experiences (209). Now his new and conniving gondoliers take him "gliding and swaying"—a forward motion at once unsteady and unhindered—through the "labyrinth" of canals where they are at home but he is, in every sense, lost. Likewise in the maze of bridges, alleyways, and "filthy culs-de-sac," under the oppressive heat and in the "stagnant malodorous air" (244). There is still beauty, but it now comes paired always with decrepitude or sordidness. There is the Oriental magnificence of St. Mark's Basilica with its glowing interior, but mingled with its heavy incense there is "the smell of the sick city" (243), the chemicals being used against cholera. Lovely blossoms trail down crumbling walls and "Moorish windows [are] mirrored in the murky water"; the marble steps of a church dip below the surface of the dirty flood (244). Beggars and dealers feign and swindle. "This was Venice, the flattering and suspect beauty, half fairytale, half tourist trap" (245).

It is now about to be a tourist trap in a literal and potentially fatal sense. If the honest travel clerk is right, visitors will soon be imprisoned in the plague-ridden city by the cordon sanitaire, which is the internationally agreed way to contain major epidemics.[1] But for the time being, the authorities, from commercial motives which are those of the swindling traders and beggars writ large, are hushing up the sickness that will be the direct cause of Aschenbach's death. To him, though, his cholera seems not a threat but a confirmation, an accomplice even, of his passion; the city has its own dark secret, and one kind of disorder winks at another. The sequence in which he uncovers the facts, from the first "uncanny" signs of "the sickness" (241) until he forces the travel clerk's full admission, is part of the tragic action's firm final line. It is also the final stage in Aschenbach's corruption, because even while he teases out the truth from those who desperately or reluctantly conceal it, he has not the least intention of using it for anyone else's good—nor, admittedly, for his own in any normal sense. He revels in the embarrassment of the people he quizzes and the alarm of those who anxiously watch it happen. For all his shocked tone when he first discovers what is going on—"'They want it kept quiet!'. . . 'They're hushing this up!'" (242f.)—he is no moral crusader. Knowledge, the guiding light of his intellectually radical younger years, now gives him a purely formal ironic superiority, the means to irresponsible play in a situation of deadly earnest. Thus when the hotel manager explains away the smells of chemical that are pervading Venice as a routine police precaution, the irony of Aschenbach's reply—"'Very praiseworthy of the police'" (247)—rebounds on him: he is as silent and therefore as guilty as the Venetians. The idea of warning Tadzio's family is something he toys with only briefly, for he has already "realised with a kind of horror that he would not be able to go on living" if Tadzio were to leave (243), as in a slightly different sense it proves. So when he imagines the "decent action which would cleanse his conscience" (255)—not to mention perhaps saving the boy's life in the process—it is like a vignette implausibly transplanted from the conventional kind of fiction where unselfish acts are performed in undisturbed awareness of lofty moral values. But Aschenbach is living at the level of instinct; he enjoys a quite different awareness, of sharing and keeping the city's guilty secret, and this only intoxicates him further. His state has already been called "drunken ecstasy" (245), and ecstasy literally means being outside oneself. An action that would sober him and "give him back to himself again" is the last thing he wants. Hence "he said nothing, and stayed on" (255), a sentence which in the German original is even shorter and denser, four terse monosyllables ("er schwieg und blieb") that stand out against the elaborate syntax all around them like an erratic block in a landscape. Their simple directness makes a subtle connection, recalling the equally simple phrase that registered Aschenbach's first response to Tadzio, his perception "that the boy's beauty was perfect" (216). It is ironic that the noble simplicity of the one has led inexorably to the brutal simplicity of the other.

Aschenbach's fate has three clearly distinguishable factors determining it: the material factor of disease, the moral factor of complicity, and the psychological factor of willing self-abandon. The narrative has traced them all and thus made a comprehensive, realistic case. But the roots of the matter go deeper, to a coherence that is not just that of modern realism. Those alien forces that have taken over Aschenbach's conscious mind, as suggested by the word *mania*, begin to be identified, indeed, they take on a personal identity: "His head and his heart were drunk, and his steps followed the dictates of that dark god [*Dämon*] whose pleasure it is to trample man's reason and dignity underfoot" (244). Though unnamed—and he will stay unnamed—the mythic identity at the center of the story is beginning to emerge.

But he has also lurked there from the first, has been present through literary allusion. Myth has all along been interwoven with realism in the sequence of figures who have marked out the route to Venice, setting Aschenbach off on it, guiding him and furthering his progress along it, prefiguring his fate. To this sequence the last chapter adds (248ff.) the grotesque and sinister street singer who performs for the hotel guests. Like the Munich figure and the gondolier, he is once more an alien type ("not of Venetian origin"), with enough of their leitmotiv features to ring a bell—hat, snub nose, prominent Adam's apple, red hair, "threatening" furrows on the brow. Missing this time are the fiercely bared teeth that in those other figures suggested a traditional death's-head. But instead there is the concentrated carbolic stench that is virtually part of the man ("he seemed to be carrying his own suspect atmosphere about with him" [249]) and is every bit as eloquent of death, for we now guess what the chemical signifies.

Unlike the distant, imperious Munich figure (but like the unlicensed gondolier), the street singer can actually be talked to at the level of realistic narrative: he answers and balks Aschenbach's questions. To that extent he crosses the gap between mythic and real, just as in the course of the scene he crosses the physical distance between performer and audience. These two movements become, indeed, almost one. As he approaches Aschenbach, the "sauciness" of the performance turns into an obsequious bowing and scraping. But once artistic distance is restored, he reasserts his own kind of authority. The uproarious dialect laughing-song that ends his act is opaque in meaning, but transparent in intention: the tables are turned on the audience, they themselves become the show, and the "humble" performer treats the spectacle of his spectators with an ever wilder and more infectious mockery until—as his ultimate triumph—he finally gets them to join in the laughter. The figure's will to power, and his sense of the true power relation between him and the audience as he manipulates their responses, are evident. At the very end of his comic exit, before slipping away into the darkness, he "suddenly discarded the mask of comic underdog" and "uncoiled like a spring to his full height." We remember the "air of imperious survey" (196) with which his Munich doppelgänger looked out from his own quasi-theatrical vantage point and faced down his quarry.

Aschenbach has not laughed. It is as if the song were secretly aimed at him and he must try "to fend off an attack or flee from it" (251); as if the mocking laughter were the voice of the "dark god" who now controls his actions, and who will shortly appear to devastating effect on another stage, that of Aschenbach's sleeping mind.

Before this high point of the mythic causal line in his dream, there is also a high point of the literal causal line, which is the detailed account of cholera. From the English clerk in the travel bureau Aschenbach learns not just the nature of the disease, its symptoms and course in the individual patient, but the history of its recent spread through Asia and Russia to the moment when it arrived in Venice. After this dense medical and epidemiological information, it will only remain for Aschenbach to contract the disease by an obvious means, the "overripe soft strawberries" (260). We will need no second telling what, at this level, he dies of. But the travel clerk's account is not just bald fact. The disease becomes in turn a symptom, of a moral failure not unlike Aschenbach's. Fear of lost tourist business has been stronger in Venice "than respect for truth" (254). The complicity of city and lover is not just an external coincidence; commercial and erotic self-interest share a common resistance to knowledge. Another link is also made. The cholera has its origins in the Ganges Delta, "that wilderness of rank useless luxuriance, that primitive island jungle shunned by man, where tigers crouch in the bamboo thickets" (252f.). This surely is the world of Aschenbach's Munich vision, the "primeval wilderness of islands" where he saw "between the knotted stems of the bamboo thicket the glinting eyes of a crouching tiger" (197). He has come "not all that far, not quite to where the tigers were" (199), but still to a wilderness of islands, merely one where the primeval has long been overlaid by a city civilization. Here something has reached out for him from that truly primeval setting he so unaccountably envisioned on his Munich stroll. The sober details and background of disease connect with something more mysterious; fact connects with fate.

Aschenbach makes no such connection himself. The sense that a pattern is coming together remains ours, not his. True, he does once look back to that moment in Munich and remembers from it "a white building adorned with inscriptions" and the "strange itinerant figure" who first awakened his longing to travel. But he does not remember the vision of jungle wilderness, and his thoughts of the building and the figure merely fill him with repugnance because they remind him of home, "of level-headedness and sobriety, of toil and mastery." Decisively, it is in this paragraph that he contemplates but rejects the "decent action" of warning the Polish family and takes a final resolve to say nothing and stay on (255). And this paragraph stands in the text between the story's two extremes: it is a border and a bridge between realism and symbolism, between the factual account of disease and the mythic dream of an ancient orgy. Aschenbach's outward acceptance of the cholera risk leads over into his deeply inward final surrender to the god of intoxication.

For the orgiastic practices he experiences in the dream are those of the ancient Greek cult of Dionysus, the god of natural growth and regeneration and rebirth, of wine and drunkenness, of collective feeling and instinct, of ecstatic inspiration. Dionysus was an "alien god" in two senses. His worship came from Asia Minor, or even, it was sometimes said, from India, and spread like a wave over Greece. But his cult was also essentially alien to Greek religious tradition, so that there was strong resistance to his invasion.[2] This is seen graphically in Euripides' drama *The Bacchae*, where Pentheus, king of Thebes, refuses to recognize Dionysus in person and even tries to imprison him. The god, naturally enough, escapes. More significantly, so do Pentheus's own deeper desires to witness the orgies of the Dionysian cult and finally to take part in them in female disguise, whereupon he is unmasked and torn apart by the celebrants (including his own mother) along with their sacrificial animals. So Euripides' play already poses the question: is the god so wholly "alien" after all, or does he not rather touch irrational impulses which are already present deep in human beings? If the god is "alien" only in the sense that human beings refuse to *recognize* those impulses in themselves—or, put mythically, refuse to recognize him and try instead to imprison him, as Pentheus does—then the story becomes a parable of what in modern times is known as repression.[3]

Aschenbach too has long practiced repression, attempted to sublimate impulse in the cause of artistic creation. It was the crisis of that practice at the start of the story that led to the question, "Could it be that the enslaved emotion was now avenging itself by deserting him, by refusing from now on to bear up his art on its wings?" (199). His whole journey has been the pursuit of liberation for that emotion, initially unconscious, then fleetingly "wondering whether . . . some late adventure of the emotions might yet be in store for him" (210), and now fully aware, overriding "art and virtue" so as to enjoy "the advantages of chaos" (255).

Even at this late stage, like the Greeks and like Pentheus, Aschenbach resists with "a profound and spiritual resistance" the forces of the alien god that have "irrupted" into his soul. But, again as with Pentheus, it seems truer that those forces were latent in him rather than external. For when the dream starts, he has no perception of himself as separate from the orgiasts' actions, "rather the scene of the events was his own soul" (255); by the end he and the celebrants are one, "the dreamer now was with them and in them. . . . They were himself as they flung themselves, tearing and slaying, on the animals" (256).

Aschenbach's Socratic reminiscences and his mythologizing on the beach were classical knowledge; they helped him to maintain some distance from his experience, to understand it in a secure context. The dream is no such comforting story chosen from his cultural resources. The graphically envisioned Dionysian orgy thrusts up from the unconscious and allows not the least detachment. The details come direct from raw experience, the "long-drawn-out final u" is not, or not just, a version of the well-known howl of Dionysian worshipers, "Io! io!"; nor is it truly "like no cry ever heard" (256). On the contrary, it clearly echoes the cry that fascinated Aschenbach, the long u of the Polish vocative that dominated the beach in the cry "Tadziu!" and now dominates Aschenbach's dreaming mind. "Loathing," "fear," the "honorable will to defend to the last what was his and protect it against the Stranger," are no match for this ever louder howling which "swelled up to an enrapturing madness" (256f.).

After his dream, Aschenbach has no resistance left. Nor does he have scruples any longer about his pursuit of Tadzio being noticed; he is concerned only about his own aging appearance. That he now has himself "rejuvenated" by cosmetics puts him on a level with the tipsy old fop who so repelled him on the boat to Venice. Less obviously, his false rejuvenation is the end of a line which began with his high aesthetic preference for the surface of things rather than the truth below it: cosmetics as the ultimate art of the false surface. Correspondingly, the three monosyllables he mutters to the voluble hairdresser who fusses around restoring his appearance harshly suggest a low point of thought and the death of verbal mastery.

Harshness might seem the story's final keynote. The pursuit of the Polish family leaves Aschenbach sweating and exhausted in an ever more deserted and stinking Venice. The narrator's tone is sardonic, even sarcastic, as he sets the writer's past prestige as a cultural pillar of the community against what he has now become. "He sat there, the master, the artist who had achieved dignity" (260): the paragraph that follows is a complete rehearsal of all those literary achievements and claims to public respect which were recorded in chapter 2. But their effect now is nullified, even reversed, by what has become of the great writer. The narrator seems intent on a total moral repudiation of his character.

Yet thought and verbal mastery are not quite dead in Aschenbach. He still has something to contribute to the meaning of his own story. It is true that the paragraph which opened with sarcasm ends by denying any such possibility. It dismisses the thought processes of which Aschenbach's "drooping, cosmetically brightened lips shaped the occasional word" as a "strange dream-logic" (260). But when the dream-logic is displayed in full, its argument proves to be both coherent and incisive. It goes back, once more, to Plato. Aschenbach has earlier remembered the doctrines of Plato's *Phaedrus* dialogue. Now he speaks as if from within that dialogue, to Phaedrus, whom perhaps he associates in his mind with Tadzio. But it is effectively a monologue: there is no answering voice. And Aschenbach speaks not as one of the characters Plato used in the dialogue, but as himself, as the artist he is and as a representative of the whole artist guild. In this capacity he makes the crucial claim that, by the very nature of artists, their difficulties in living up to Plato's ideal are especially, even uniquely, acute.

This short, dense section of text interweaves the Platonic doctrine of beauty with the particular shape of Aschenbach's career right down to its last stage of deterioration; it draws the conclusion that there simply was no right path for him. Whatever he did—and, more generally, whatever any artist does—must be tragically wrong in one direction or another. The analytical knowledge of which he was once a devotee, "sympathizes with the abyss," it even "*is* the abyss." Yet to turn away from that abyss (which was the point of Aschenbach's "profound decision") and become instead a devotee of beauty only leads to another abyss. For it means seeking the spirit through the senses—and can that ever be free of risk? His musings put this as an open question to the imagined Phaedrus, a trick that Socrates, as the intellectual hero of Plato's dialogues, typically uses when the conclusion he is working towards has become unmissable but he wants his interlocutor to be humbled by admitting it: "Or do you think (I leave it to you to decide) that this is a path of dangerous charm, an errant and sinful path which must of necessity lead us astray?" (267). The answer is not in doubt. So it seems the flight from one extreme, one abyss, can only lead to another. But this is not just a confession, it is the modern artist's answer, dressed in Platonic pastiche, to Plato and his doctrine of a transcendent reality: a defensive plea that if beauty really is so over-whelmingly present to the senses, then the artist, of all people, simply cannot rise above it or go beyond it. To do so would be to deny its—and his—fundamental nature. The risks of beauty are rooted deep in his calling. Artists, such is Aschenbach's sweeping generalization, "are not capable of self-exaltation, only of self-debauchery" (261). It is a gloomy conclusion. (But then Plato, who wanted no art or artists at all in his ideal republic, would scarcely have been surprised.)

The scene, plainly, goes beyond literary realism. Suddenly the Aschenbach who just now was at the end of his physical and moral tether is lucidly drawing the lesson from his almost completed tragic fate and passing a categorical judgment on the possibilities—or rather, the impossibilities, the impasse—of the life and commitment of writers. It is a coherent overview, an exact and bitter recognition. And precisely this coherence and persuasive quality reflect back on the dismissive way the narrator introduced Aschenbach's thoughts, as "strange dream-logic." If the logic seems neither strange nor in any pejorative sense dreamlike, then not only was that label inappropriate, but perhaps everything about that paragraph—the judgment it contains, the sarcastic tone, the moralistic emphasis—was far from being the last word either. Perhaps they were some kind of narrative feint? For by now we are used to the idea that a style can be false, even a façade, and one of Aschenbach's conclusions in these Platonic musings is that "the magisterial poise of our style is a lie and a farce" (261). And one of the things the false style of his "deliberate classicism" went in for was emphatic moral judgments that "weighed vileness in the balance and found it wanting" (204). So when the narrative voice at this late stage in the story practices just such a moral emphasis, it is strangely, almost obtusely, untouched by what the story has taught us about the hollowness of self-confident moralizing. By now, surely, this and any uncomprehending contempt has only a very shaky claim to legitimacy.

Because for anyone who has eyes to see, the story has traced back Aschenbach's moral attitudes and actions to their aesthetic causes, the causes in turn to the course of his career, and the career to cultural pressures. These, for all his conscious "profound decision," shaped the consciousness that did the deciding. We *understand* Aschenbach too well by now to be able simply to repudiate him, and that means accepting that his fate is tragic. He himself in his maturity rejected the whole notion of understanding, and the forgiveness that proverbially goes with it, because of "the laxity of that compassionate principle" (204). Wanting to have and give simple moral assurance in a complex world, he restored such traditional concepts as that of a "vileness" which could be straightforwardly weighed and found wanting. That left no room for tragedy, which since the time of Aristotle has been largely defined by the compassionate understanding it arouses: showing the fearful necessity of a human being's fate, it invokes our pity. The irony is that Aschenbach's moral fall puts him in need of the compassion he once scorned. The narrative has made the case for it, and at the end he himself comes to see the necessity with which his fate unfolded: "We necessarily go astray, necessarily remain dissolute emotional adventurers" (261). The refusal of understanding rules itself out of court, and with it all overconfident moralizing, whether Aschenbach's, which events have discredited, or that of the sarcastic narrator. Strikingly, Aschenbach is not above pleading his own cause. His whole Platonic speech is a discreet way of appealing to our sympathy. For when he addresses an imagined and silent Phaedrus, the effect is as if he were directly addressing us; though outwardly his speech has the detached wisdom and gestures of superiority which we associate with a Socratic teacher ("Mark well . . . I must tell you"), its substance is a frank description of his own case. Didactic authority here rests on confessional authenticity—it is the one source of authority Aschenbach does have left, just as the only lesson he can teach is the impossibility of pedagogy, and even that only to an imagined pupil.

But the story's tragic understanding goes still deeper, is more complete, than Aschenbach's own. When he uses Platonic categories to understand the case of artists generally, he is strangely silent about the "alien god" who was the driving force and climax of his own. He speaks of "intoxication"—that much is now clear to him—but not of its lord. Though he has experienced Dionysus directly in his dream, has awoken from it a definitively changed man, "unnerved, shattered, and powerlessly enslaved to the demon-god" (257), yet he seems not consciously to know him. (The only god he does name, true to the conceptions of the Platonic dialogues, is Eros.) Perhaps he has suppressed or lost his knowledge of Dionysus in the transition to waking life or subsequently. That would repeat the pattern of his Munich vision, and with it those other instances in Mann's fiction when a character is granted a dramatic vision but soon, realistically enough, forgets it (see above, p. 31f.). So if Aschenbach's late reflections have brought him back to the analytic knowledge he once turned his back on, it is only a partial knowledge. He tells himself a story that is not quite the full story. For deeper even than the Platonic problem he ponders there lies the Dionysian element, the ultimate source of passionate feeling and potential destroyer of order. Aschenbach's conscious mind has not plumbed that abyss.

Even the insight he does achieve comes too late, in the same way that each successive advance of knowledge in the course of the story came too late: the recognition at the close of chapter 3 that parting from Tadzio was what made leaving Venice so painful, or the recognition at the end of chapter 4 that he is in love with the boy. Both these partial recognitions are wisdom after the event, only possible once the event cannot be reversed. They are thus more like appendages to the action than integral parts of it. In the same way, the last and fullest recognition contained in Aschenbach's monologue is in both senses a conclusion. It is the product of a development which is now essentially complete and cannot be affected by it.

The story's ending, after the drama and degradation of the Dionysian dream, after the sarcastic moral judgment, after the Platonic meditations, is very matter-of-fact. The brief narration of Aschenbach's actual death feels like a coda. The foreign visitors have heard rumors and gone, it is prematurely end-of-season, the beach is autumnal and bleak; a photographer's tripod stands there deserted. There is also a different feel about Aschenbach's final sight, or rather vision, of Tadzio—no more the desperate pursuit that led up to his moment of truth in the little Venetian square, no more the sensuously perceived idol, nor even the aesthetic form celebrated earlier. Yet the close too has a touch of the unreal, and we can choose (as so often with Thomas Mann) either to accept it as a suprarealistic effect or to put the sense of unreality down entirely to the fevered mind of the character, as the phrasing allows—"to him it was as if . . . as if . . ." (263). The real boy who has just suffered humiliation at the hands of his long-subordinate companion moves off to sulk; he becomes unreachable not just for Jascha but in a new way for Aschenbach too. He is "a quite isolated and unrelated apparition . . . in front of the nebulous vastness." And where once his beauty had blocked off any view of a spiritual Beyond, he now positively points—or it seems to Aschenbach that he points— beyond himself and out to sea, "outward, into an immensity rich with unutterable expectation." So when the sick man tries to get up from his deckchair and follow "as so often," he is no longer pursuing an object of desire but following the directions of a "soul-summoner," a mythic guide on a journey beyond Venice (263).

The final paragraph with its three laconic sentences registers Aschenbach's death and in so doing propels us abruptly out of the claustrophobic Venice setting. His death is the end of a private history, but it is also a public event in a world that has no knowledge of that history. For this world, his reputation remains intact. So it can be "respectfully shocked" at the passing of a still unquestioned master.

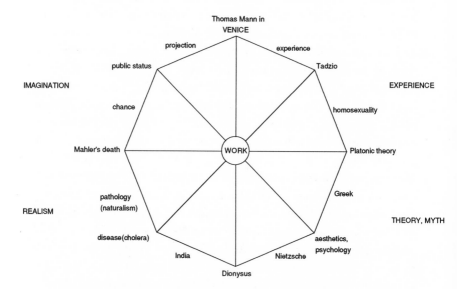

The diagram is a simple attempt, suggested by Thomas Mann's image of *Death in Venice* as a "crystal," to show both the story's thematic richness and the unplanned connections which its events, figures, motifs, and ideas turned out to have. These separate elements are named at the points of the octagon, while the nature of the connection between each and its neighbor is suggested by the label against the line that joins them. For example, reading anticlockwise from the apex, *Mann in Venice in 1911* is linked to (Aschenbach's) *public status* by imaginative *projection*; while a sense of what it is like when an artist of such status dies comes from the *chance* that *Mahler's death* occurred during Mann's journey. In the other direction, the link with *Tadzio* is through Mann's Venice *experience,* and the connection with the next point onwards, *Platonic theory,* is via *homosexuality*. And so on. The connecting process comes full circle, and the elements with their connections feed into the work at the center. Each quarter of the octagon also groups the elements by a general affinity, which is indicated in CAPITALS. These four concepts represent the large and disparate areas which the story succeeds in bringing together.

9

Connections, Genesis

In his *Sketch of My Life*, published in 1930, Thomas Mann picks out two things about the writing of *Death in Venice*. One is that the novella had a will of its own which carried it well beyond the meaning he intended to give it. The other is that the resulting text, which had formed spontaneously like a crystal, was more than usually multifaceted and rich in connections; and the notion of "connections," he says, is for him central to the very idea of significance.

These two things, the story's "will" and its richness of reference, are in the end only one. For it was precisely the way objects and events turned out to have interconnected meanings—meanings not planned but discovered as he wrote, an "innate symbolism"—that gave him at times a feeling he says he had not known before of being "carried serenely along" by the work's own impetus in a kind of "absolute movement" (XI, 123f.). As the connections emerged, the novella composed itself.

That is not to say that it *wrote* itself; the act of writing was as laborious as always for Thomas Mann, with doubts and shifts and despairs. But the process of composing—literally, "putting together"—a pattern of meanings could seem at least in retrospect as if it had been achieved by the materials of the story themselves and the many associations they brought with them. These came, moreover, from disparate sources, yet they proved to be compatible, sometimes by the most remarkable coincidences. The result was literary meaning that was complex but not contradictory: actual experience turned out to have potentially rich associations within the complex codes of culture. For a writer who from his beginnings had striven beyond the narrow limits of Naturalism, this was a deeply satisfying demonstration of how much more could be latent in mere reality than was accommodated in Naturalism's view of the world.

Yet the process by which those associations "came together" and "proved compatible" took place over time, not in a single revelatory instant. To that extent Thomas Mann's image of a sudden crystallization is misleading. The significances of the novella were a matter of accretion and interaction, of clarifying the relations between elements, while all the time the author's changing attitudes were reshaping his materials and his theme. The story has a story; its genesis shaped its significance.

Should we probe behind the product for the process? The text warns (though, of course, it ignores its own warning): "It is as well that the world knows only a fine piece of work and not also its origins"— i.e., Tadzio as inspiration for the last page and a half of Aschenbach's career—"for knowledge of the sources of an artist's inspiration would often confuse readers and shock them, and the excellence of the writing would be of no avail" (236). Yet arguably the opposite is true of Aschenbach's own story. *Death in Venice* works its way through intricate aesthetic and moral issues and is shaped by the phases in which its author worked his way through them. Knowing "the conditions under which it came into being" may actually sharpen our understanding of the issues and make the writing of more, not less "avail." To live always only with resolutions is to forget what problems are.

VENICE

Not the least significant thing was the location itself. In 1911 Thomas Mann traveled to Venice with his wife Katia and his brother Heinrich.

Like Aschenbach, he was escaping from a difficult stage in his current work which had temporarily exhausted his nervous energies (letter to Heinrich Mann, 24 March 1911). He had been to Venice before, and its fascination for him must always have been intensified by its background of associations with figures he admired to the point of passion. Richard Wagner had composed part of his *Tristan and Isolde* there in 1858—his autobiography, just published in 1911, made much of that phase—and had died there in 1883. Friedrich Nietzsche had stayed there and written evocative poetry about the city, also published only recently in his autobiography *Ecce Homo* (1908). And the homosexual poet August von Platen—a favorite writer for Mann, who knew many of his poems by heart—had been there in the 1820s and published the set of eloquent *Sonnets from Venice*. Platen too died in Italy, in flight from Venice and a threatening cholera epidemic. The city could hardly have been closer to Thomas Mann's most private culture through its associations with homoeroticism (Platen), with things decadent (Wagner), and with the ambition to overcome them (Nietzsche). Through these and many other links, as well as through its sheer bizarre extravagance, Venice had for some time been the favorite city of Europe's "decadent" writers generally: "No other swamp creates such violent fevers," wrote Gabriele d'Annunzio, not at all in a critical spirit.[1]

But when things with a seemingly "innate symbolism" happened to Thomas Mann in Venice, the city ceased to be just cultural background. It became a source of specific motifs that would interweave with the "adventure of the emotions" that Aschenbach looks forward to when his steamer arrives off Venice. This passage is itself an example. As anticipation stirs in the traveler, it is Platen he remembers and recites to himself; the text half quotes a sonnet of Platen's which celebrates the first sight of Venice's buildings rising from the waves (210).[2] Indeed, linking Aschenbach's expectations with the well-known homosexual poet makes almost too strong a motif, or at least a premature one—if, that is, we are to believe that Aschenbach's first admiration for Tadzio is innocently aesthetic. Later, when he is pursuing the boy through the labyrinth of canals and the narrative reminds us how the arts "once rankly and voluptuously blossomed" in this "insalubrious air" and "composers were inspired to lulling tones of somniferous eroticism" (245), the reference to Wagner's richly sensuous music is also no longer cultural background but part of the case that is being built up against art's elevated claims. And Nietzsche. . . . But Nietzsche is everywhere in the work, dictating its terms and pervading its substance.

NIETZSCHE: PSYCHOLOGY AND MYTH

Nietzsche claimed to be the greatest living authority on decadence, on the grounds that he was both a decadent himself and its very opposite,[3] i.e., a critic of his age and a vehement preacher of psychological and cultural health. It was avowedly from him that Thomas Mann learned the "psychology of decadence" which shaped the inward "decline of a family" in *Buddenbrooks* (XI, 556). This, though, was only part of the early debt. In the 1890s the young Mann immersed himself in Nietzsche, whose writings were a cult that swept all before it. Mann's thinking was marked from an early stage by Nietzsche's first book, *The Birth of Tragedy from the Spirit of Music* of 1872. Its scholarly aim—Nietzsche wrote it when briefly a professor of classics at the University of Basel—was to show the dynamic that underlay Greek tragedy. Against the clichéd view of the ancient Greeks as statuesquely serene figures in an ideal Mediterranean landscape, he evoked the forces they had to hold in balance before their art could come about. That meant giving full value to the violent primal impulse in human makeup as well as to formal control. Beyond the matter of Greek tragedy, this was a dramatic pre-Freudian picture of the necessary tensions that underlie all culture. And like Freud, Nietzsche brought abstraction alive by embodying it in the figures of myth, in his case, the Greek pairing of Dionysus and Apollo. Dionysus was the god of fundamental productive and destructive energies, of nature, spring, regeneration, wine and intoxication, who drew human beings by their inchoate drives into the collective and allowed them to glimpse the tragic realities of existence; Apollo was the god of light and artistic form who shaped those drives and insights into the clarity and order of dream, individuality, a detached art. The affinities of Dionysus were with music, the art of direct emotional overflow, not representation of some external object; Apollo's affinity was with the firm, clear outlines of sculpture. When these contrary but also complementary impulses were held in productive tension, they gave Greek tragedy its power and plasticity. Dionysian experience gave it its depth; Apollo's shaping hand gave it its form. The beauty of the finished work made life bearable despite its tragic nature; art created an illusion that was psychologically necessary if life was to continue. Paradoxically, the Greeks as creators of beautiful forms—including their gods—were "superficial because they were deep."[4]

Yet surely, Nietzsche thought, the Dionysian and Apolline impulses, and the forms they were capable of generating, were not peculiar to the Greeks? If they could only be brought into balance once again, they might regenerate late-nineteenth-century German culture, which in his view badly needed it. It was excessively cerebral, and its creativity was weighed down by the accumulated knowledge and reflective consciousness of an "advanced" civilization—a diagnosis which meant incidentally that Germany needed Dionysus more urgently than it needed Apollo. In the music dramas of Wagner, whom at this stage Nietzsche idolized, he saw his hopes of an artistic rebirth and a new tragic culture for Germany already on the way to being fulfilled.

Nietzsche's is a powerful and graphic account of art and of the forces that go into its making. It also points up fundamental problems. Imbalance between the two elements will clearly lead to artistic failure. Too much Dionysian energy unchecked by Apolline form, and the work of art will be chaotic; too much Apolline control without a Dionysian impulse to tax and extend it, and a bloodless formalism will result. Nietzsche's theory also implies dangers for the maker of art. (It can scarcely be expected that something as valuable as great art will be risk-free.) For the artist, keeping the two impulses in balance, harnessing them through a discipline of work and integrating them in a manageable way of life, will itself be a creative act. If the balance is lost and the discipline breaks down, there may be a serious crisis. When Aschenbach and his narrator join in that early question—"Could it be that enslaved emotion was now avenging itself by deserting him, by refusing from now on to bear up art on its wings, by taking with it all his joy in words, all his appetite for the beauty of form?" (199)—they are glimpsing (though Aschenbach does not pursue the insight further) the loss of that essential balance and integration. In the vision he has just had of a rank, luxuriant jungle and the beast of prey lurking there, what has stirred in his unconscious is the attraction of the wilder primal impulses which his years of discipline have kept too strictly subjugated. Even before this, the very first sight of the stranger has made him "conscious . . . of an extraordinary expansion of his inner self." That is exactly how the effect of Dionysian possession was described in the scholarly work on which Thomas Mann drew for his knowledge of the cult.[5]

So even this early in the narrative there is already a discreet mingling of psychology and myth. The two things may seem to us fundamentally different ways of understanding human behavior. Psychology sees it as resulting from inner processes, myth represents it as obeying the external compulsion of a god or following the set pattern of an archetypal story. Yet the one mode can embody the other, as it had already done in Nietzsche's originating essay, and long before him in the mythic creations of the culture he was analyzing: "We appropriate these names from the Greeks, who made the profound mysteries of their view of art accessible to anyone with insight, not in concepts, but in the strikingly clear figures of their gods" (*The Birth of Tragedy*, sect. 1). *Death in Venice* proceeds similarly. It links the psychological and the mythic modes from the start and represents an inner breakdown as the thrilling yet vengeful visitation of a god. For it to do this, the reader only has to sense the special quality of that first ominous figure in Munich. Exact identification is not needed. It is enough, to start with, if the bizarre confrontation lifts events and our response to them out of the ordinary, if the bared teeth suggest a death's-head. That sensitive the novella's title should already have made us. The bared teeth of later figures will confirm the intuition of something extra-ordinary. Aschenbach's first gondolier may be recognized as a ferryman across death's river, and perhaps even, with a very modest knowledge of ancient mythology, as Charon. His curt "'You will pay'" (214) is a strong hint, a touch too ambiguously threatening to be merely part of the realistic narrative. Other recurrent details—the broad-brimmed hat and the staff, the physical appearance and attitudes—may be noticed by the reader later and may be seen as attributes of Hermes, guide of souls to the realm of the dead, or of Dionysus himself. The more precise the identification, the more our experience of the work is enriched and unified along the lines of Thomas Mann's syncretistic conception. But even short of precise identification, importantly, the reader may still sense the function of the recurring figures, which is to give narrative coherence to the process of psychological breakup that has already begun in Munich and whose consequences the journey spells out.

But if psychology and myth are two ways of talking about that one process, why does cholera enter into it as the literal cause of death? On the face of it, only because there was a cholera epidemic in Italy in the summer of 1911. But what Thomas Mann called "innate symbolism" then makes its connections. Cholera originated in India, spreading across Asia and penetrating Europe from early in the nineteenth century. And it was from India that the religion of Dionysus was traditionally said to have come, spreading (as Thomas Mann's sources put it) like an epidemic[6] across Asia Minor and Greece. So Aschenbach's vision of a jungle swamp contains the causes of his destruction at more than one level: psychological—it is a metaphor of his repressed impulses ("The moralist hates the primeval forest," wrote Nietzsche, taking it as a symbol for "the whole previous history of the mind and those of its possibilities that have not yet been drunk to the lees"); mythic—it is a place associated with the god of those impulses; and naturalistic—it is the source of the fateful disease. Similarly with the lurking tiger. He is at home in the literal jungle where cholera originates. But he is also a Dionysian animal: tigers drew the god's chariot in the myth. What is more, the tiger, along with lions and leopards, is a metaphor of the primal and primitive which crops up frequently in German writing around the turn of the century, a further debt to Nietzsche and the vocabulary of his vitalism.[7]

HOMOSEXUALITY: GREECE VERSUS WILHELMINE GERMANY

The release of a writer's repressed impulses did not have to mean homosexual passion. Mann's first idea for the theme of lost dignity in a great writer, around 1906, was a heterosexual subject: the episode of the old poet Goethe falling in love at 74 with a girl of 17. This belongs, strictly speaking, more to the prehistory of *Death in Venice* than to its genesis. It is a quite different conception and has only one thematic strand in common with the one that replaced rather than grew out of it, namely, late loss of dignity through sexuality. Its main interest lies in the contrast it offers: it allows us to see just how much richer and more unified a conception grew out of what happened in Venice. As in the case of the cholera motif, outward events brought inner complexity with them unbidden, especially through the homosexual element. The writer's admiration for young male beauty allowed the further theme of blindness or self-deception. (There was no self-deception, or possibility of it, in Goethe's attraction to the young Ulrike von Levetzow.) Aschenbach's failure or refusal to recognize his own feelings could then be connected with his mature rejection of self-knowledge, and at the same time with the new aesthetic priority he has for some time been giving to visual beauty, an Apolline ideal under cover of which Dionysian feeling can get a hold. (Paradoxically, the more total the commitment to Apollo, the more complete the later surrender to Dionysus.) And since these new aesthetic directions of Aschenbach's were career temptations of Mann's own, the subject Venice offered him had the potential to capture his whole literary situation. And not just in any detached way. This was an actual "adventure of the emotions" for him to come to terms with, more real and more pressingly immediate than a mere anecdote from some famous past life, especially one from a writer's old age which for obvious reasons it would have been difficult for Thomas Mann to identify expressively with. The tale of Goethe's late infatuation was in any case grotesque rather than serious, material for something perilously close to a routine debunking of greatness.[8] In contrast, the erotic excitement Mann apparently experienced in Venice brought home to him the precariousness of private morality and public reputation in a real and threatening way.

Not that the impact of young male beauty was the surprise for Thomas Mann that it is, when at last he recognizes it, for Aschenbach. Mann was well aware of his own sexual ambivalence. His attachment to the painter Paul Ehrenberg had been the great emotional experience of his life in the years that led up to his marriage in 1905. *Tonio Kröger* of 1903 was in a sense addressed to Paul Ehrenberg, designed to show him that inside the cool ironist he thought he knew there was a sensitive and suffering human soul. But if that is the background to Tonio's yearning for acceptance by Hans Hansen, the literary treatment remains very discreet: homoerotic feeling is there only as a boyhood phase, followed in the normal sequence by Tonio's crush on Ingeborg Holm. There is a similar sequence or mixture in later works like *The Magic Mountain* and *Felix Krull*. Mann's feelings for Paul Ehrenberg were not transposed directly into fiction until many years later, in the Leverkühn-Schwerdtfeger relationship of *Doctor Faustus*, and discreetly enough even then. Thomas Mann's ambivalence about his own ambivalence prevented him from being the kind of pioneer his French contemporary André Gide became, with the confessional frankness of the novel *L'Immoraliste* (*The Immoralist*, 1901) and his autobiography *Si le grain ne meurt* (*If it die*, 1921), and the equally explicit arguments of his dialogue *Corydon* of almost exactly the same date as *Death in Venice* (printed—but in only 12 copies—in 1911, published fully in 1924 [see "Über die Ehe," X, 196]). Thomas Mann, by contrast, remained as timid and reticent in fiction and autobiographical statement as he did, on the evidence of his diaries, in real life.

Except, that is, this once. The emotions inspired by his Venice experience—or (to say no more than we can know for certain) its power to inspire persuasive images of what a consuming passion would be like—produced one of the rare classics of homosexual feeling.

But how affirmative a treatment could it be? Here "literature" meets "society" head-on. For if, on the one hand, the writer had an intimate and challenging experience to convey, on the other he had the expectation, or rather the near-certainty, that the result would meet with little sympathy. This was Europe not long after the trials and imprisonment of Oscar Wilde (1895–97). Gide in France, we saw, felt he had to hold back his *Corydon*. In Germany, accusations of homosexuality had recently (1902, 1906) caused scandals and a suicide at the highest levels of Wilhelmine society, reaching up to the kaiser's own circle.[9] If we add this larger background to that of Thomas Mann's stay in Venice, it seems likely that he turned to Plato for sympathetic confirmation from a society of very different outlook, as well as for deeper insight into his experience and its implications. Ancient Greece, certainly Athens at the time and social level of Plato, so the *Symposium* and *Phaedrus* suggest, had not been hostile to homosexuality in the way modern Europe was. Even four centuries after Plato, the Platonic tradition was alive in Plutarch's dialogue *Erotikos*, where the relative value of homosexual and heterosexual love is still being argued out as an open question. Mann was to draw on that work too—a new translation appeared opportunely in 1911.

But the Greek texts did not offer mere cozy reassurance; they set austere standards and creative aims for the lover. If Nietzsche's theory of Dionysian and Apolline impulse provided the story's dynamics, the Greek dialogues provided its ethics. Mann's work notes include substantial passages transcribed from all three dialogues, and there is no hint that they have been gathered and are being deployed merely as materials from which to construct Aschenbach's alien responses and reflections. With no framework of critical comment, they look as if they are there simply for the light they throw on the nature and possibilities of homosexual feeling.

Its possibilities for literary creation, barring some distinct moral failure in the lover, were plainly great (see above, p. 55f.). What is more—and this makes a connection between the two kinds of Greek source—the same was potentially true of the Dionysian force. For despite the destructive violence of his cult, Dionysus is also a god of regeneration and new growth. In psychological terms, freeing the writer's long pent-up and overexploited emotions might have meant literary rejuvenation. So far, so good. What is more, journeys in literature commonly transform the traveler. That, unobtrusively, is the pattern in *Tonio Kröger*: the writer achieves renewal by a journey back to the roots of natural feeling, albeit only to its social roots and through very much gentler adventures. Add to this the fact that Mann himself had got safely back from Venice without being destroyed by passion or disease, and was once more writing freely; not, it is true, on the *Felix Krull* project, which he had been unable to push further at the psychological low point before his vacation, but on the Venetian subject itself, the story of a (for better or worse) transforming passion. It is not clear why it had to be for worse, why it had to be death in Venice rather than new poetic life. Yet when Aschenbach writes with Tadzio there before him on the beach, we are firmly told, not that he feels elevated and spiritually fulfilled, but that he feels debauched and that his conscience accuses him after it.

This is the pivotal point in the story and in the conduct of its moral argument. How much so is clear if we remember an earlier moment, and the potential it suggested. It is the scene where the sight of Tadzio running out of the sea inspires "mythical images" in Aschenbach's mind (224), and he feels "song" stir inside him. No mere trivial ditty either, but *Gesang*, the word used in German for high poetry. At that point there is no necessary obstacle to literary renewal. There is perhaps even a hint, in the combination of Tadzio's statuesque form and Aschenbach's inward song, that the Apolline and the Dionysian are being brought together.

That the outcome did not absolutely have to be tragic, and that the novella might have followed a very different line and still been faithful to Mann's Venice experience (including its regenerative effect on him) and to his classical sources is not just a matter of gratuitous speculation. For his later accounts of how the story was written suggest that a more affirmative work did nearly come about. These retrospects of Thomas Mann's testify to the nature and power of his original inspiration, but they also confess its—or to be more precise, his—limitations.

The first of these retrospects is in verse. It is the opening of his only nonprose work, the *Song of the Child* of 1919, and the unfamiliar situation of composing in verse leads him to reflect yet again on what kind of writer he is. One episode and its bitter lesson sticks in his mind:

Remember? Intoxication, a heightened exceptional feeling
Came over you yourself on one occasion and threw you
Down, your head in your hands. To hymnic impulse your
                    spirit
Rose, amid tears your struggling mind pressed urgently
                    upward
Into song. (VIII, 1069)

He is speaking of the very beginnings, the Venetian beginnings it
would seem, of *Death in Venice*; the dominant note of this recollection
several years after the event is regret at a literary failure. He speaks of
an "ancient shame" and a "secret defeat," even though the novella that
resulted won great public acclaim. For despite his "intoxication," he
could not sustain the "hymnic impulse" which, for once in his sober
prose-writer's life, had begun to generate "song" (once more the word
in the original is the elevated *Gesang*). "Unhappily," he goes on:

                    things stayed just as they had been:
    There began a process of sobering, cooling, and mastering—
    Lo! what came of your drunken song was an ethical fable.[10]

In other words, having been (almost) carried away, he went back to
being the kind of writer he had always been, the morally aware, intellectual, analytical *Schriftsteller*. It was another failure to win what he
had always coveted and so often been refused by critics: the status that
German usage denotes but never quite defines when it confers the title
"Dichter." The word literally means "poet," though it connotes not
verse but literary quality and public acceptance. For example, at the
end of *Tonio Kröger* the title figure, and with him no doubt his author,
had looked forward to achieving that status through a new emotional
commitment to ordinary life.[11] In his notes for the essay "Intellect and
Art," Mann had tried various arguments: now to claim the title, now
to challenge the German ways of thinking that gave it its special aura.
And in the first upsurge of what was to become *Death in Venice*, he
perhaps felt the title within his grasp, only to see it elude him once

more. If anything could have secured it, it was surely a work of impassioned inspiration—perhaps for good measure in verse too, which is what particularly recalls it to his mind as he begins to write *Song of the Child*. Now he can only try to cut the Gordian knot of that old issue and claim that the title of "Dichter" ought by rights to be his on the strength of his work as it always has been and still is:

> for where from the outset his love of a language
> Joins with all other loves and mingles with all that he
> goes through,
> Let us be bold and give the writer this name—he deserves
> it.

Yet clearly the old failure to follow that original Venice impulse still rankles. As he presents it, the failure sprang from a deep-rooted literary character. But intertwined with issues of literary form, social scruple was also at work, whether fully conscious or internalized as a taboo. This second element does not have to be guessed at, since it is part of the explanation Thomas Mann gives in a second retrospect which is probably the fullest and frankest self-interpretation he ever penned.

Mann's letter of 4 July 1920 to the young poet Carl Maria Weber is meant to remove any impression the novella might have given that "a mode of feeling [that is, homosexuality] which I respect because it is almost necessarily infused with *mind* (far more necessarily so than the 'normal' mode) should be something that I would have wanted to deny or, insofar as it is accessible to me (and I may say it is so with scarcely any reservation), would have wished to disavow." He tries to locate the possible causes of misunderstanding. The first is, in the story's own Nietzschean terms, "the difference between the dionysian spirit of lyricism whose outpouring is irresponsible and individualistic, and the apolline spirit of objectively committed, morally and socially responsible epic narration." In other words, a passionately felt private experience is all very well for lyrical poetry but will and must be toned down before being put in front of the public in prose narrative. That is, it would be irresponsible not to tone it down, and such toning down is an intrinsic part of epic form.[12] Hence his striving after "a balance of sensuality and morality," a morality that would off-set the sensuality of the work. Yet this, he says, cannot hide the fact that "at its core" it is "hymnic in character, indeed of hymnic origin," and he quotes the lines from *Song of the Child*, already discussed above, which evoke the Venice experience and his first response to it. If those lines mean that he began by writing in verse, then the occa-sional full hexameter and the numerous fragments of hexameters that critics espied long ago[13] embedded in the prose of *Death in Venice* may be remnants of such a first form. That makes it the more sadly apt that Mann should have recorded the defeat of his efforts at hymnic song in a different "song" composed in hexameters. Apt and ironic, since *"Gesang vom Kindchen"* is as far removed as possible from the cele-bration of homosexual love. It celebrates the christening of his sixth child.

Mann calls the process of cooling into prose "the *artistic* reason" (his emphasis) for what then looked like an unsympathetic attitude to homosexuality. But the social element is strong, and explicit. He told Weber there were also what he calls "purely intellectual" reasons, though in fact these are in some measure artistic: "the *naturalistic* atti-tude of my generation, so alien to you young people, which compelled me to see the 'case' *also* in pathological terms (the climacteric) along-side and mingling with the symbolism of Tadzio as Hermes psy-chopompos." But then, he confesses, there was the most deeply personal element: "the absolutely un-'Greek,' the fundamentally protestant, puritanical ('bourgeois') character which I share with the story's protagonist; in other words, our deeply mistrustful, deeply pes-simistic attitude to passion itself and in general."

The letter continues and becomes almost an essay, moving out from the themes of *Death in Venice* to the larger context of Mann's intellectual world at the time he wrote it, and the place of homosexual feeling and its artistic products within that world. His overriding aim is to defend the novella against the charge of being negative. But alongside this defense and the virtual full confession of his own homo-sexual feeling there is an equally clear confession of the limits—artis-tic, social, personal—beyond which he could not or would not go. The full force of Dionysus was not something for society, or for prose fiction, or for this particular prose writer. Those constraints were plainly crucial in making the story what it became.

Perhaps no more was needed to transform the "hymnic" conception, despite its Platonic possibilities—which are strikingly not even mentioned in the letter to Weber. But well on in the writing of the novella, reservations about Plato were added to those about Dionysus. An essay by Georg von Lukács published in 1911,[14] probably autumn, analyzed Plato-Socrates' cultivation of yearning as a principle of spiritual growth, but frankly declared such yearning to be hopeless: it could have no spiritual fulfillment on earth, so it was forced to take on the lower forms for which some sort of fulfillment is possible. Lukács writes of men and of poets that "their exaltation is always tragedy. . . . In life . . . yearning must remain love: that is its happiness and its tragedy." That pessimism is the keynote of Aschenbach's speech to Phaedrus near the close, and formulations from Lukács's essay can be recognized in Thomas Mann's text, the wording in each case pushed to a more drastic extreme. "Our yearning must remain love,—that is our pleasure and our shame." And, "We are not capable of self-exaltation, we are capable only of self-debauchery" (261). Hence Thomas Mann's conclusion in the work note (no. 4) that contains his excerpts from Lukács: "Dignity can be saved only by death ('tragedy,' the 'sea,'—recourse, rescue and refuge of all higher love)." This image of a sea into which the lover would move out may have been long in his mind as a possible ending for the novella, but perhaps in the positive sense of Plato's "sea of beautiful forms" to whose shore the true initiate comes, to be pointed onwards by the single being that first inspired his love. That passage from the *Symposium* (210d) is transcribed in Mann's work notes (no. 16). But in the finished story, there is no suggestion, or certainly not a firm one, that Aschenbach has achieved any such initiation. "Sea" has become instead the real Adriatic beside which he dies, at most a symbol for the uncertain promise of death into which Tadzio beckons his lover on.

If death it was to be, then the feel of those moments when a great figure departs this life was also by chance one of the experiences of Thomas Mann's Italian journey. In the summer of 1911 Gustav

Mahler had just returned gravely ill from an American tour, "and his princely decline into death in Paris and Vienna" could be followed "step by step in the newspaper bulletins" (XIII, 149). The hushed respect of that occasion whispers in the novella's last line.

Since *Death in Venice* is a complex story about complex issues, it ought not to surprise anyone to find that its genesis was also complex. Like the plot of the story itself, the genesis is a history of conflicting impulses within a writer, some universally human, some specific and individual, some internalized from the surrounding culture. The whole mixture was inherently unstable. That as well as the delicacy of the subject is why Thomas Mann more than once while writing it spoke of an "impossible conception"; was still stuck for an ending at a stage when arrangements to publish were well advanced; was desperately concerned to complete the story somehow; and then, when at last it was finished, did not know what to think of it.[15]

All this hardly fits Mann's image as the most sovereignly intellectual among modern writers. That is no great loss. Intellectualism is neither a sufficient nor a necessary quality in a writer. Ideas and reflection may put much into the melting pot out of which the work comes, and clearly did so in this story, but the work itself cannot be wholly planned. Encounters with experiences and ideas remain unpredictable and challenging. A writer so intellectual as to have everything immutably cut-and-dried would simply be out of live touch with the things that matter enough to make literature, and that make literature matter to us. Being, on the contrary, *in* touch meant being carried by the complexities of the work, not just in the beneficial sense of Thomas Mann's comments with which this chapter began, but in the sense of being moved in different directions by the pressures of subject and sources and society and his response to all of them. It is then an achievement if the writer can in some degree master and unify the mixture. "Mastery," in other words, cannot result merely from the ambitious planning of "great works," such as occupied Thomas Mann in the years before 1910, any more than it had been able to result from the laborious working up of slight motifs into disproportionate structures—the dialogues of *Fiorenza* that ponderously overstate an idea already more briskly done in *Gladius Dei,* or the allegory of *Royal Highness* which spends 350 pages elaborating Tonio Kröger's parallel between the artist and "a prince walking incognito among the people" (157). Those really *are* products of "intellectualism." To create works that are less perfunctory, less predictable, there must be something that demands to be shaped, that extends the author's capacities of mind and verbal skill beyond plan and intention and leaves the text as its necessary trace. That this was so in *Death in Venice* sets it apart from the works, written and unwritten, of Thomas Mann's doldrum years.

There is more than one reason for wanting to trace the processes that shaped a work of art. Such inquiry helps us appreciate the work as an achievement, and it also sharpens our understanding, both of the text and of its reception: for example, the shifts of authorial position that led Thomas Mann at different times to claim the text's qualities for himself as "classical" and to disclaim them as conscious "mimicry,"[16] or those inner contrasts of tone which have made one critic suggest the novella has "two authors."[17] There has sometimes been resistance to any following up of Thomas Mann's genetic hints.[18] Yet to do so is not a gratuitous practice, and certainly not a matter merely of conjecturing stages prior to the final text, but rather of feeling the full force of the text itself. Thomas Mann, after all, did not tell Weber only that the work was of "hymnic origin," he said the finished text itself still *was* "at core hymnic in character." Unlike his later image of a crystal, which is apt for the work's many facets, the image of a core still visibly present despite outward changes exactly fits those passages where a "Platonic" lyrical enthusiasm has had a moral framework built immediately around it.[19] And on a larger scale, chapter 2, interpolated (when?) into the narrative line and already implying the outcome of the experiment, provides an analogous moral framework for the whole novella. We know what psychological and social pressures made these frameworks necessary, just as well as we know what emotions created the dangerous core they were designed to surround. This ambivalence is the key to understanding the style and structure of *Death in Venice.* In a sense the story did indeed have "two authors," but neither of them was the kind of bloodless artificial narrator-construct modern criticism routinely assumes when analyzing narrative. They were alternating personas of the real author himself, whose motto could well have been the words of Goethe's Faust: "Two souls, alas! dwell in this single breast."[20]

By 1930, as we saw, Thomas Mann could look back on a confusion from which he had climbed free, could recall that his novella had surprised him about himself, and could say that it meant more than he had meant it to mean. That makes the situation sound settled. It was firmly—was it not?—a moral fable, and safely part of the past. But the story's story was even then not ended. The growth of its meaning still had some way to go.

10

History: or, What Dionysus Did Next

History is almost the first note *Death in Venice* strikes: the world in which Aschenbach takes his afternoon walk is overshadowed by a threat to the peace of Europe. But from that point on, the narrative treats an intensely inward subject that has no obvious link with public events. Aschenbach is admittedly a public figure, and the story's outcome suggests how precarious and doubtful such a status is. But this is presented first of all as a psychological and moral problem in the individual artist's life; in its widest application, it concerns the mutual relation between writers and the community that reads and respects them, a social but hardly a historical matter. The story thus seems at first sight to be continuing Thomas Mann's obsession with the artist's (that is, ultimately, his own) problems, an obsession that excluded almost everything else, and certainly excluded public affairs and events, from his artistic vision of life before the First World War. Typical of this is the passage of *Tonio Kröger* where the artist—and the narrative is taking him seriously, not showing him up as unduly self-absorbed—tells Lizaveta Ivanovna that "no problem, none in the world, is more tormenting than the business of being an artist [*das Künstlertum*] and its effects on human beings" (158).

Most readers nowadays will respond to that statement with incredulity and quickly call to mind a whole clutch of problems—social, political, moral—that are both more "tormenting" and more obviously "in the world" than the self-concern of a fictive, and behind him an actual, artist. After that opening reference to the threat of a European war in some unspecified year early in the twentieth century, the historical note is not struck again. It thus seems to have been a purely decorative motif, or at most a way to set Aschenbach's private destiny in a framework of larger menace, part of the deliberate solemnity of a narrative which, we saw, uses omens to create suspense and suggest tragic necessity.

Yet the novella does bear on German history in an indirect way. Besides being filled with ominous figures and happenings, *Death in Venice* is also a kind of omen itself. Rather than reflecting the history of its own time or an earlier time, as works of literature are commonly thought to do, its connection is with events that still lay far in the future when it was written. They obviously therefore could not affect the author's literary intention. But this may only make the story's historical reference the more real and the more impressive.

What the novella turned out long afterwards to have uncovered (or so it seemed to Thomas Mann) was an important root of Nazism. In Aschenbach's attitudes and decisions, with their tragic private consequences, hindsight showed Mann a pattern which on a larger scale had helped to shape politics, with devastating public effects. It was not simply, or even particularly, the Prussian-ness of Aschenbach's discipline of life and work and its fragility, on which the Marxist critic Georg Lukács put such historical emphasis.[1] After all, if "Prussianism" specifically was significant in German history, it was through its continuity, not its breakdown. Thomas Mann's psychological insight went deeper. His story traces the fate of an all-too-conscious master-artist who has grown impatient with psychology and analysis, desires a simplified view of the world and the human mind, attempts a new "resoluteness" beyond moral complexity—and as a consequence has no defense against destructive self-abandon. These elements of a powerful anti-intellectual syndrome were, so Mann wrote in 1938, very much tendencies of the time, they were in the air long before the word "fascism" existed, and are scarcely recognisable in the political phenomenon that bears that name. Yet in spirit they are in some measure connected with it, morally they served to prepare the way for it. I had these tendencies in me as much as anyone, I included representations of them here and there in my work, for example in the formula of a "reborn naïveté" in the drama *Fiorenza* [VIII, 1064; cf. 204]. What I wanted to point out in our conversation was simply how understandable it is that I must hate and despise the depraved shape reality has given to spiritual things I carried in me twenty, thirty years ago.

This in a letter of 30 May 1938 to his American friend and patron Mrs. Agnes E. Meyer. It had come as a shock to her when Mann in conversation first made the link between fascism and his own work. How could anything in the intellectual history of this great humane writer be even remotely connected with the vileness of Nazism? In the America of the thirties, what is more, he was the foremost German exile spokesman against the Nazis. As events moved towards war he was trying to raise American consciousness of what Nazism meant and to break down isolationist attitudes. Surely (it must have seemed to Mrs. Meyer) it took an excessively sensitive moral conscience to link himself with that regime, even with its remotest intellectual history?

Yet Thomas Mann was refusing, precisely, to do what Aschenbach had done with such tragic results, namely, to be uncomplicatedly "resolute" and to adopt his fictional figure's "morally simplistic view of the world and of human psychology" (205)—refusing to do so even now, in a historical situation which seemed to make simplification permissible if ever it could be. Though his writings and broadcasts of the thirties and forties are entirely resolute in using the "massive power of the word" against Hitler's Germany, and though he was later to call the Nazi period a "morally good time" because it made moral priorities plain (XI, 253f.), still it was only in a historical emergency and for the most urgent political purposes that it was proper to divide the world into black and white, good and bad. It was not an option for the more complex view that is characteristic of art or of historical understanding.

So when in 1939, the year after his exchange with Mrs. Meyer, Thomas Mann wrote the essay "Brother Hitler" (XII, 843), he brought out precisely the features that were common to himself and the man he most cordially hated. Perhaps he was already groping towards a grand historical fiction of his time and obscurely felt that it would only be possible to grasp its spiritual history if he went beyond simple moral outrage at what had happened, however justifiable in this case moral outrage might be. In retrospect, Mann saw himself as part of that history, sharing responsibility for it as a German, specifically as an artist and intellectual, and more specifically still as the kind of artist he had been. What had occurred in Germany was not a takeover of the good by the bad, but the distortion of a single culture from within. The thread needed careful untangling.

That is the message of Mann's lecture "Germany and the Germans," given at the Library of Congress in 1945 (XI, 1126). The message is then immensely and movingly elaborated in what he called "the novel of my epoch," *Doctor Faustus*. He began it in 1943, with the Second World War still raging, and published it in 1947. It traces the dilemmas and temptations to which the twentieth-century German mind, individual and collective, was exposed, dilemmas and temptations that are shown to have affected both the subtleties of art and the currents of public thought and feeling that prepare political change. Thomas Mann sees the symptoms everywhere: impatience with the seeming dead-end of European civilization; a consequent rejection of basic concepts like justice and truth; a deliberate retrogression into instinct and unreason; a preference for primitive rather than refined methods in the most diverse areas. This willing self-abandonment is presented in Thomas Mann's chosen myth as a surrender to ultimately demonic forces—*Doctor Faustus* is, of course, a remake of the German moral fable of Faust. But it is also a remake, enlarged and intensified, of his own "moral fable," *Death in Venice*, even though his new protagonist is a musician, not a writer. Thomas Mann says in one of the work notes for *Doctor Faustus* that he has long carried the idea for a

"Faust" about with him (it was first sketched in a notebook of 1905) and that "deeper moral associations have accreted." Some of them came from *Death in Venice* and from later reflection on the themes he had treated in the novella. This is implied in the same note, which diagnoses the deepest impulse of his modern Faust figure, Adrian Leverkühn, and of the nation he allegorically represents, as "the desire to escape from everything bourgeois, moderate, classical [added: "Apolline"], sober, industrious and dependable into a world of drunken release, of bold, dionysian genius, beyond society, indeed superhuman." And this "intellectual-spiritual fascism" is further diagnosed as a "dionysian denial of truth and justice."[2]

These preparatory notes for *Doctor Faustus* show how different a degree of prior clarity Thomas Mann brought to the later work. And in line with this, the new protagonist shares his author's awareness of contemporary processes—intellectual, psychological, artistic—even while he is living through them. Where Aschenbach had been drawn on all unknowingly from a change in his approach to art, via a crisis in his productive routine, to an encounter which is first revivifying and then destructive, Adrian Leverkühn in contrast sees with total lucidity his own place in the history of music, understands the impasse of modernity, knows that only drastic means will get him out of it, embraces (in realistic terms) syphilitic infection, or (in mythical terms) a pact with the devil, and makes inspired music from the pathologically heightened condition ("intoxication") that finally leads to his mental collapse. A parallel is pointed with the equally pathological condition (in literal terms) or the devilish pact (in mythic terms) through which Germany gained its brief intoxicating triumphs of the thirties and forties before the collapse and defeat of 1945. Figures, major and minor, and other motifs link the late novel with the earlier novella. But the fundamental relation is between on the one hand a work that captured a tendency of its age all unknowingly as a seismographic trace, and on the other hand the mature analysis that knows how to read it. In other words, where *Death in Venice* is a historical document, *Doctor Faustus* is a work of history. But so accurate does the document seem to its author that it decisively marks the ideas and structure of his most ambitious novel. In this respect too *Death in Venice* is what Thomas Mann called it, an experiment, one on whose results he later felt able to rely.

To help understand Thomas Mann's feelings of complicity in German guilt, we have to go back and see stage by stage just how, and how far, he participated in the historical processes of his time and place. If irrationalism is the villain, then long before *Death in Venice* there were the self-doubts of the artist and intellectual Tonio Kröger, seemingly harmless in his wistful self-subordination to "Life" and the simple value of "normal" people. This lyrical masochism or "self-betrayal of the intellect" (XII, 26) has its roots in the late-nineteenth-century notion that artistic and intellectual activity arises from decadence, cultural value from the decline of vital forces. How could any artist embrace his calling and its associated values wholeheartedly when it was a widely held belief in his society (and, as a child of his time, he believed it himself) that they arose from vital deficiency? This is the motive for Mann's flirtation around 1910 with allegedly postdecadent efforts at "regeneration" (but what could have been more decadent than such hectic overcompensation?), as documented in his notes for the essay "Intellect and Art." Much of the complex of problems and temptations manifest in those notes, but left unresolved as a set of issues he could not yet master, went into the imagined career of Aschenbach. Aschenbach, besides completing other unfinished projects of Mann's listed in the first paragraph of chapter 2, has finished his equivalent of that essay and solved the equivalent of those problems, it is evident in what way. His tragic history duly shows the perils of the anti-intellectualist position that he thereby arrived at: what happens when you think you have achieved a "reborn naïveté," when you become morally resolute, deny analysis, reject "the abyss," and devote yourself to an unproblematic beauty of the surface.

If the novella was indeed an experiment, and if tragedy was its outcome, then that hard-won conclusion ought to have warded off all such temptations for good. Yet in the years immediately following, something like Aschenbach's impulses reassert themselves, admittedly in a very different outward guise. Within two years of the appearance of *Death in Venice*, the "grave threat" to the peace of Europe which haunts its first paragraph was fulfilled. From the start of the First World War in August 1914, national emotions and basic instincts seized even the most sophisticated citizens of the European combatant nations. Writers and intellectuals were no more immune to war fever than anyone else. With few exceptions, they supported not just war but the national policies that had led ever more inexorably to war. Thomas Mann was prominent and vocal among them. This is not the place to analyze general causes or attribute political guilt. The striking thing for present purposes is the way Thomas Mann's internal development had long since assigned him his place in an embattled Germany with a logic that was clear to him, though it came as a shock to those few literary colleagues (not least his brother Heinrich) who stood out against the nationalistic fervor. They declared themselves astonished that he, renowned as the cool intellectual, the detached ironist, did not join them. Yet in fact this greatest of all societal stresses, war, was precisely the signal and pretext to come into the fold that Tonio Kröger, with his longing for "life in its seductive banality" (163), had needed. In an essay of autumn 1914 called "Thoughts in War," Thomas Mann rejects intellect, critical consciousness, and civilization as shallow and "western" in contrast with a German culture which is altogether profounder and nonrational and therefore compatible with such primitive practices as "pederasty" and "orgiastic cult forms" (XIII, 528). In these wild utterances we can hear obvious echoes of *Death in Venice*, as well as of arguments left unresolved in the notes for the never finished essay "Intellect and Art." We can also recognize in them Tonio Kröger's suspicion of intellect and longing for the "bliss of ordinariness," but driven now to feverish extremes by the atmosphere of the first months of conflict. Near the end of the war, and of the massive work of self-justification and polemic that he spent the war years writing, *Considerations of an Unpolitical Man*, Thomas Mann himself makes the link between the yearnings of that novella and his (to some) unexpected political behavior. He quotes a long passage from *Tonio Kröger* to explain why he, the intellectual and outsider, necessarily leapt to Germany's defense in 1914. He was championing a community which for him represented "Life," and the

clue had been there for all to see in his celebrated story of ten years
earlier:

> I wrote: "It is absurd to love Life and nevertheless to be trying
> with all the skill at one's command to entice it from its proper
> course, to interest it in our melancholy subtleties, in this whole
> sick aristocracy of literature. The kingdom of art is enlarging its
> frontiers in this world, and the realm of health and innocence is
> dwindling. What is left of this realm should be most carefully pre-
> served: we have no right to try to seduce people into reading
> poetry when they would much rather be looking at books full of
> snapshots of horses." It can be seen that I was applying those
> words and concepts to moral and intellectual things, but uncon-
> sciously there is no doubt a political will was alive in me, and it is
> again clear that one doesn't have to be a political activist and
> demonstrator, that one can be an "aesthete," and still, at a pro-
> found level, be in touch with things political. (XII, 586, quoting
> VIII, 303 [Luke translation, 162; cf. 140ff.])

It is a perceptive self-analysis. The bonds of communal feeling had
been waiting to be pulled tight by some great crisis like war. But it is
easy to see how for Heinrich Mann, as a critic of German actions and
of the Wilhelmine society that had generated them, the national pas-
sions of his brother and other intellectuals called to mind a different
story. In his essay "Zola" of 1915, overtly about the French novelist's
conflict with the state over the Dreyfus case but alluding constantly to
Germany and its intellectuals in 1914, Heinrich wrote that "it is the
fate of reason periodically to grow weary, to abandon itself, and to
surrender the field to the orgies of a complicated naiveté, the out-
breaks of a deep and ancient anti-reason." The phrasing here recalls,
no doubt deliberately, the Dionysian orgies in *Death in Venice*, which
are ultimately the result of Aschenbach's "complicated naiveté."[3] It
was certainly not implausible to see the collective emotions of intellectuals in time of war as a deeply Dionysian phenomenon.

The wartime controversy between the two brothers estranged
them from each other for almost a decade; they were not reconciled
until 1922. But Heinrich's reading of the politics of 1914 as a manifes-

tation of atavistic impulse was then virtually taken over by Thomas as a key to understanding the rise of fascism in the twenties and thirties. Most observers concentrated on the externals, the "normal" political factors that had brought this extreme movement into being. There was the unpopularity of the Weimar Republic among Germans, which sprang from its origins in the traumatic defeat of 1918 and the way a new form of state was felt to have been imposed on Germany by the victors. There was the resentment many felt (and were incited to feel by right-wing politicians) against the Versailles Treaty, which had imposed punitive reparations payments and contained a clause recognizing Germany's exclusive guilt for the First World War. The instability of the Republic was also thought to stem from its frequent changes of governmental coalition and its repeated economic crises (the reparations burden, the hyperinflation, the consequences of the Wall Street crash). Altogether, certainly, few modern states have had to contend with such pressures and with such fierce internal opposition, from left as well as right, not just to the specific government in power but to the republican form of state itself.

Thomas Mann did not discount any of these things, but he believed they were only the occasions, not the essence, of fascism. They were the surface conditions that served to let loose deeper and darker forces in German society—and also (which undercut the standard explanation of German fascism from purely German circumstances) in other European countries. Mann was speaking of Europe generally when he wrote in 1925: "The anti-liberal backlash is more than clear, it is crass. It shows itself politically in the disgust with which people turn away from democracy and parliamentarism, turning faces of dark resolve towards dictatorship and terror" (IX, 166). This political development seemed to him at root an irrational acceptance of primitive forms, and not just an unconscious one. The fascist ideology drew on a tradition of explicit irrationalism—Nietzsche, Klages, Sorel, and others—to scorn and attack rationality, reflection, the critical mind, and any group that was committed to these things: the hated West, the hated intellectuals, the hated Jews. (For propaganda purposes, the three groups were easily and deliberately confused with each other.) Against the liberal values such people represented, fascism embraced and preached a tribal irrationality. The political consequence was an uncritical, near-ecstatic submerging of individuality in the collective which nobody who has seen original newsreel of an Italian or German fascist rally will think it far-fetched to call intoxication.

But was it right to call it a Dionysian intoxication? Or was that unnecessarily to dishonor an ancient deity and a vital element in the human makeup? In a letter to Thomas Mann of 13 August 1934, the mythologist Karl Kerényi, just back from observing at firsthand the behavior of young Germans, called it "a bad, non-dionysian (I might say dysdionysian) madness." The originator of the term "Dionysian," Nietzsche himself, had at first distinguished between the Dionysian element in Greek tragic culture and a cruder barbaric version found elsewhere in the ancient, and indeed the modern, world. In this other version, "the wildest beasts of nature were unleashed, to the point of a loathsome mixture of voluptuousness and cruelty" (*The Birth of Tragedy*, sect. 2). Later, fatefully, Nietzsche lost sight of this distinction and his revulsion against barbarism receded, to be replaced by an undiscriminating enthusiasm for cruelty as a sign of cultural health, most notoriously in his celebration of the "blond beast" of primitive warrior-nobilities. And in notes towards unfinished works just before his writing career ended in insanity, he asks with positive longing, "Where are the barbarians of the twentieth century?"[4]

By the late 1920s the barbarians had arrived. Nearly every essay Thomas Mann wrote and nearly every speech he made in the years up to 1933, whatever else its topic and whatever its thesis, is also a dismayed response and a call for opposition to the new irrationalism in German political behavior and what passed for German thinking. His Berlin speech of 1930, "German Address: An Appeal to Reason," is the high point and summary of his commitment. To borrow the phrase with which he had described Aschenbach's weighty responsibilities, Mann himself was more than ever "preoccupied with the tasks imposed on him by . . . the collective European psyche" (198)—now in the most literal sense, because the European psyche had become "collective" to a terrifying degree. To see and say what was going on in its depths required a psychopathologist, and it is a bitterly apt comment of Mann's that in the Nazi annexation of Austria in 1938 Hitler's real target was a certain aged analyst working in Vienna.

This reminds us that Mann's mode of explanation for fascism was not unique to him. In his *Civilization and Its Discontents* of 1930, Freud similarly saw the patterns of social behavior determined not by influences operating on the social surface, but by forces deep in the psyche. In the postscript to his *Autobiographical Study*, he declares that "the events of human history . . . are no more than a reflection of the dynamic conflicts between the ego, the id and the super-ego, which psychoanalysis studies in the individual—they are the very same processes repeated upon a wider stage."[5] Carl Gustav Jung argued much the same, especially in his thirties essay "Wotan." And as early as 1924, D. H. Lawrence wrote a "Letter from Germany" that conveys a sense of terrible regression, of "time . . . whirling with mysterious swiftness to a sort of death. Whirling to the ghost of the old Middle Ages of Germany, then to the Roman days, then to the days of the silent forest and the dangerous, lurking barbarians."[6] The letter was not printed until ten years later, when events had confirmed Lawrence's extraordinary insights. Mann's diary entry for 19 October 1934 registers an unsurprising approval: "Admirable what a sure eye for essentials in Lawrence's letter about Germany and its return to barbarism at a time when Hitler was not yet even talked of."

But fascism was not just an alarming factor in the outside world, to be treated only in essays and speeches. In 1929 Mann published *Mario and the Magician*, the tragic-grotesque study of an audience under the hypnotic sway of a brutal yet subtle performer. Set in Italy, it is both an atmospheric literal record of the new national assertiveness fascism had promoted in national communities, and an allegory of fascism itself with its brutal yet subtle propaganda methods. But the central figure, Cipolla, is also a kind of artist, and there are hints that he works with Dionysian means, achieving "a drunken dissolution of critical resistance" in his audience and driving them to an "orgy of dance" (VIII, 700f.).

By the time of his exchange with Mrs. Meyer, then, Thomas Mann could look back over this whole history in which *Death in Venice* was the most telling document. Despite his honorable resistance to the irrational in its gross Nazi form, he could feel disquiet at being part of the culture of an age that had veered so sharply towards irrationality, at seeing how closely his own work had been involved in that trend and thus "in touch with things political" in a much grimmer sense than his words of 1918 intended.

This deep disquiet is the driving force behind the confession that *Doctor Faustus* contains. Unless we are cynical enough to suspect that Mann's confession is just a last fling of Mann's self-centeredness, a desperate effort to get into the historical act at any price, then in the light of his overall political record it must seem the act of an unduly sensitive conscience. Yet it deserves to be taken seriously for at least two reasons. One is its consistency. It is the logical conclusion of a life's work which itself took seriously the part ideas and psychological forces play in human affairs; Mann's need to confess his own real involvement was the acid test of that belief. The other reason is its ethical value. When a historical evil that pervaded a nation comes to its end, most of those who have been involved rush to exculpate themselves and to accuse others. People rewrite history to prove that they were the innocent victims and point the finger at the guilty agents. Self-justification is the rule. Self-scrutiny and confession are the exception, the more sorely missed because they might have offered a more promising route back to social normality. In that respect, *Doctor Faustus* is not just a great and complex novel, it is an exemplary human act.

Whatever view is taken of that, it may at least now be clear how *Death in Venice* relates to the politics and history of Mann's lifetime, and how far the life story in which it stands gives a larger sense to Tonio Kröger's claim that "no problem, none in the world, is more tormenting than the business of being an artist."

Appendix: A Selection from Thomas Mann's Work Notes for Death in Venice

[*This appendix is meant to give the reader some sense of what "sources" and "influences" mean in the concrete detail of Mann's compositional practice, and of how they look to the scholar in their raw state. I therefore provide no cross-references either within Mann's text or to his sources. The highly motivated reader may try tracing them independently, e.g., in the dialogues of Plato and Plutarch discussed in chapter 7 and listed in the Bibliography. The less motivated but still interested reader can find them ready-traced in the critical editions also listed there. For the full German text, see Primary Works in the Bibliography.*]

1. Tadzio's smile is the smile of Narcissus seeing his own reflection— he sees it in the face of the other person, he sees his beauty in its effects. This smile also has something of the coquetry and tenderness with which Narcissus kisses the lips of his shadow.

4. *Connections from Ch. II to V*
   Forebears, sterling service
   Love of fame and *capacity* for fame.
   "See it through." Discipline. War service. Under the tension of great works. The "Despite" principle.
   Ascent of a problem-individual to dignity. And now! The conflict is: from a position of "dignity," from a hostility to knowledge and

second naiveté, from an anti-analytic condition, he gets involved in *this* passion. Form is sin. The surface is the abyss. How acutely for this artist who has achieved "dignity" art once more becomes a problem! For the artist, Eros is the guide to things intellectual, to spiritual beauty, for him the path to the highest things passes through the senses. But that is a path of perilous delight, an aberration, a path of sin, although there is no other. "Poets will always be denied this kind of noble exaltation. Their exaltation is always tragedy. . . . In *life* (and the artist is the man of life!) yearning must remain *love*: that is its happiness and its tragedy."—Realisation that the artist *cannot* attain dignity, that he necessarily goes astray, remains a bohemian, a gipsy, a libertine, an adventurer of the emotions. The composure of his style appears to him as lies and foolishness, decorations, honours, ennoblement highly ridiculous. This dignity can be saved only by death ("tragedy," the "sea,"—recourse, rescue and refuge of all higher love).

The artist's fame a farce, the trust of the masses sheer stupidity, education through art a risky undertaking that should be prohibited. Ironic that boys read him. Ironic that he has become "official," been ennobled.

6. "Only beauty is at one and the same time visible (perceivable, bearable by the senses) *and* delightful," i.e. a part of the divine, of eternal harmony. . . . We would be destroyed by the others, as Semele was. Thus beauty is the way of the sensuous person, the artist, to what is "delightful," divine, eternal, harmonious, intellectual, pure, ideal, *moral*: the only path and—a perilous path, which almost inevitably leads astray, leads to confusion. Love of beauty leads to what is moral, i.e. to the rejection of sympathy with the abyss, of psychology, of analysis; leads to simplicity, greatness and a fine austerity, to a reborn naiveté, to form, but precisely thereby back to the abyss. What is moral? *Analysis?* (The destroying of passion?) It has no austerity, it is knowing, understanding, forgiving, without composure and form. It has sympathy for the abyss, it *is* the abyss. Or *form*? Love of beauty? But it leads to intoxication, to desire and so equally to the abyss.

8. *Madness as the correlative of form and measure.* Known among the Greeks: at the time of their fullest development *madness* (μανια), a temporary disturbance of psychological equilibrium, a condition in which the conscious mind is overwhelmed, a state of *possession* by alien forces, gained far-reaching importance as a religious phenomenon. This overflowing of emotion has as its opposite pole in Greek religious life: the calm and measured feeling with which heart and gaze are raised to the gods.

Home of the cult of Dionysus is *Thrace.* Celebrated on mountain-tops *by night, by the light of burning torches.* Noisy music, *the crashing of brazen cymbals, the thundering of great hand-drums, and the deep tones of flutes whose "harmony lures to madness."* The inspired celebrants dance with wild exultation in furious, swirling, stumbling circles over the high fields. Mainly women, in long flowing garments sewn from fox-fur or with deerskins over them, with horns on their heads too, with streaming hair, snakes in their hands, and *brandishing daggers or thyrsus staves, whose points are hidden under ivy.* Their *wildness goes to the extreme,* they finally fling themselves on the animals chosen for sacrifice, hack and tear and bite off the bloody flesh, and swallow it raw. And so on.—The aim is mania, over-excitation, rapture, excess of emotional stimulation to the point of visionary states. Only through over-excitation and expansion of their being can humans achieve contact and connection with the god and his hosts. *The god is visibly present or at least near, and the din of the festival is meant to draw him fully to them.*

Ekstasis. Hieromania, in which the soul, escaped from the body, is united with the divine. It is now with and in the god, in the state of *enthusiasmos.*

9. *Daemon* as a name for the higher powers as a whole, especially when it was thought something unfavourable could be attributed to the deity, particularly a *bewitchment of the human being to do evil,* even in a satanic way. The daemon who *drives the man of noble striving into error and transgression* is the deity in person.

Dionysos: His significance is far from exhausted with the delights of wine and intoxication; he can offer quite different excitements and thus corresponds to a large area of ancient life, indeed of human nature generally, about which the ancients never spoke explicitly.

The mask of the hellenic fertility god conceals a half-alien being. One of the personifications of the "suffering" (dying and resurrected) god, whose cult was celebrated with excited lamentation and jubilation, had taken on in Asia Minor too and among the Phrygians and Thracians a particularly wild, noisy activity, and in repeated intrusions had substituted himself for the Greek Dionysus. The god is described as an *alien, intruding violently from outside....*

10. In response to this experience he yields up all at once the last remnant of his strength and his capacity for intoxication. Exit raving.

Mercury had the task of guiding souls down to the underworld and hence was called psychagogos and psychopompos.

12. In the market-place of Chalcis the monument to the Pharsalian Cleomachus, who won victory for the Chalcidians and died with his beloved (darling) looking on. The Chalcidians, who had previously loathed pederasty, after this heroic deed began to esteem it particularly and hold it in high honour....

The bravest peoples, the Boeotians, Lacedaemonians, Cretans, were most given to love, and just as many of the ancient heroes, e.g. Meleager, Achilles, Aristomenes, Cimon, *Epaminondas. Along with the last-named his darling Caphisodorus fell at the battle of Mantinea* and lies buried beside him.

14. "For the friend is more divine than the beloved. The friend bears the god in himself."

15. *From Agathon's speech: "But the god is young and his figure is delicately formed....* Where he meets with a rough response, Eros flees, and he will dwell only in the gentle soul.... And finally, do we not know *that in the mastery of the arts too only that person shines and is admired whom Eros has taught*, and that all those the god has not touched remain in the shade and without fame? ... Eros is the creator of all tenderness, voluptuousness, grace and yearning among

mankind.—In all labours, in every fear and every desire, *in the word—* there he is a sure guide, there Eros is a help and rescue."

16. ". . . and so in the sight of this multifarious beauty let him no longer yearn like a slave for the beauty of this one boy and desire the beauty of this one human being, and be common and petty . . . but rather, *arrived at the shores of the great sea of beauty*, here create many noble words and thoughts with the *inexhaustible urge to wisdom*, until then he is strong and mature and has a vision of that unique knowledge, which is the knowledge of the Beautiful. . . . Yes, Socrates, the person who, because he was able to love the beloved in the right way, begins to make the ascent from below and to see that eternal beauty, *that person has come to the end and is perfected and initiated. . . .*

17. *Phaedrus.* "Whenever anyone catches sight of something beautiful here on earth, he remembers the true beauty, and his wings grow, and he would gladly fly back to it. . . . *And is considered as one possessed.* But I say to you, this divine bliss is genuine like no other."

[. . . . .]

"The uninitiated and corrupt man is not easily brought to the sight of beauty when he sees an earthly copy. He is blind and not capable of *reverence* . . . indeed, he does not shrink from sexual enjoyment and is without shame in his unnatural desires. But when the initiate, one of those *who looked much upon beauty in that higher realm*, sees *a face of divine semblance, which mirrors that great beauty*, or the beautiful form of a body, then he trembles and a sacred fear comes upon him as it did before. . . ."

18. Infinity compressed into one, perfect beauty standing on the earth, captured in *one* human figure.—Intoxication and adoration.

He sees the eternal forms, Beauty itself, the unified ground from which every beautiful form springs.

20. Eros and *word.* (In the word—there he is a sure guide. Relationship of the eloquent Athenians to him. Writing on the beach.)

Only that person shines in art whom Eros instructs. His art too was a sober service in the temple of Thespiae. Eros has always been in him. Tadzio was always his king. His love of fame too was Eros.

22/24. *Cholera asiatica*

The mortality rate varies according to the severity of the epidemic and to how old the patients are. It reaches 60–70 percent. About half the population is immune.

Since a long way back the disease has been native to certain parts of Eastern India. Since 1817 it has shown a striking tendency to spread to other countries. In 1816, scattered smaller concentrations developed in the Ganges estuary. In the following year the disease *spread* over the whole sub-continent, by the end of 1818 it had already *taken in* the whole of Eastern India, *devastated* the islands of the Indo-Chinese archipelago, in 1820–21 it *spread* over the whole of China and by 1823 it had *penetrated* via Persia as far as Astrakhan. . . .

[*This is the start of a lengthy note sequence—it makes some six printed pages—on the history of cholera, the symptoms and course of its various forms, the details of the Hamburg epidemic, and the means of combating the disease.*]

Hygiene:

In Italy in accordance with a law of 1865 there is a Health Council under the Minister of the Interior, a Health Council in every province, one in each district, and Health Committees in the municipalities.

International regulation on quarantine measures: set going for cholera by congresses, among others one in 1892 in Venice. States undertook to inform each other immediately cholera was discovered, and further settled the nature and extent of surveillance of persons when cholera threatened, and especially of affected or suspected ships.

Quarantine:

People who have fallen ill with cholera-like symptoms may be detained, others only medically examined (at the customs point). Travellers arriving from an affected place are subjected at their destination to five-day surveillance by the medical authorities.

The *Ganges* flows into the Bay of Bengal, forming together with the Brahmaputra the largest delta in the world. The south of the delta, a luxuriantly overgrown *very unhealthy* swamp and island labyrinth, is called the *Sunderban*.

$$\begin{array}{r} 1911 \\ \underline{-53} \\ \text{born } 1858 \end{array} \qquad\qquad \begin{array}{r} 1858 \\ \underline{30} \\ 1888 \end{array}$$

23. [*Newspaper cutting with a profile photograph of Gustav Mahler.*]

26. Development of his style: towards the classical and settled, traditional, academic, conservative.

Alongside the cloistered tranquillity of his outward life, extreme blasé fastidiousness of his nerves through art. (And through the adventures of his material: bloody episodes in the Frederick novel.)

As far removed from the banal as from the eccentric.

"*Despite.*" His works achieved not only against the pressure of his delicate constitution, but also against his *mind*, against scepticism, mistrust, cynicism directed at art and artists themselves. The heroic Hamlet.

27. District Court, Provincial Court, Provincial Court of Appeal.

Liegnitz 66,620 inhabitants. Garrison. Provincial and District Court. Grammar School.

His type of hero

Gustav Mahler

Courtesy of the Thomas Mann Archive, Zurich.

Poetry only to begin with, then prose writer

Problematic youth: scepticism about artists and their world. Knowledge, irony. Then increasing dignity.

30. [*Newspaper cutting on a current cholera epidemic in Italy, from the* Münchener Neueste Nachrichten *of 5 September 1911.*]

31. Begins to follow him. (By day he pursues him without a break, at night he watches—.) (Love gives the lover freedoms—to become a slave.)

Pandering Venice.

On what paths!—Tries to get a moral grip. Remembers his forbears, his courageous life. Eros and bravery. New impressions of the "sickness." The manager. The musician. The Englishman. The epidemic.

Complicity.—Wild dream of the alien god.

Broken nerve and complete demoralisation. Hair coloring and waving. Pursuit through a sick Venice. The strawberries. Realisation by the cistern. Last view and dissolution.

Notes and References

Where works are referred to in abbreviated form, full details are given in the Bibliography.

Chapter 1

1. Mann had in mind mainly such painters as Franz von Lenbach or Franz von Stuck. His argument about the "superficiality" of all visual art is itself superficial if applied to greater artists, like Rembrandt or Van Gogh. There is no sign Mann had noticed the avant-garde painters in Munich—Wassily Kandinsky, Franz Marc, Paul Klee, August Macke—who formed first the New Artists' Association and then, in the year *Death in Venice* was begun (1911), the Blaue Reiter group. See Kolbe, *Zauber*, 212ff. It is a tantalizing question whether Mann knew Douanier Rousseau's painting *Le Rêve* of 1911, where jungle and tiger are the dream vision of the female figure, as they are of Aschenbach in chap. 1 of Mann's novella. (Reproduced in Schmidgall.)

2. An entry in his earliest preserved notebook quotes a French aphorism, "To think that everything has been discovered is to take the horizon for the limit of the world," and comments, "Naturalists please note!" *Notizbücher 1–6*, 21.

3. Note 10. The full German text of Mann's notes for this never completed essay ("Geist und Kunst") is printed in Scherrer and Wysling, 152–223.

4. See the letters to Heinrich Mann of 27 February and 23 December 1904, which have a strong element of self-justification.

5. See Thomas Mann, *Notizbücher 7–14*, 120.

6. Ibid., 186.

Chapter 2

1. "German Books: Thomas Mann," *Blue Review* (July 1913), reprinted in D. H. Lawrence, *A Selection from Phoenix* ed. A. A. H. Inglis (Harmondsworth: Peregrine, 1971), 283.

2. Cf. letter to Paul Amann, 10 September 1915: "The most embarrassing thing was that people interpreted the 'hieratic [i.e., high-priestly] atmosphere' as personal pretension, whereas it was nothing but mimicry" (*DüD* 1, 406). Elsewhere (e.g., letter to Josef Ponten, 6 June 1919, *DüD* 1, 412) Mann uses instead the more common literary term "parody."

3. Mann became aware of this paradox himself. In his 1940 Princeton lecture "On Myself" (XIII, 150) he speaks of "a strange *dual-track quality* [*Doppelgleisigkeit*—italics his] in poetic thinking" such that he had been able in an essay to claim that literature is a valuable guide for young people, whereas in a story he had drawn savagely pessimistic conclusions about any pedagogical role for artists and writers. What Mann does not draw attention to is the important point: which of these things came first? That is, the story does not retract the opinion (which would be a normal enough sequence); rather the opinion is reasserted after and despite the tragic findings of the story.

Chapter 3

1. There are three good surveys (all in German) of the response to *Death in Venice*. They overlap only partially in content and approach. Vaget, *Kommentar*, provides a condensed description; Bahr, *Dokumente* the most substantial extracts; and Böhm, *Selbstzucht*, the sharpest argument. Full references for articles which I mention only by author's name are given in the above volumes.

2. See the section "Maximin" in the volume of George's poems *Der siebente Ring* (1907), especially the poem "Kunfttag I"; and also his foreword to *Maximin: Ein Gedenkbuch* (1906). George's comment on *Death in Venice* must have been privately reported to Thomas Mann, probably by his friend Ernst Bertram, who was a member of the George circle. Mann quotes it in the important letter to Carl Maria Weber discussed in chap. 9.

3. See chap. 2, n. 1.

4. O. Zarek, "Neben dem Werk," reprinted in *DüD* 1, 411f.

5. First argued in the earlier of the two critical editions of *Death in Venice* listed in the Bibliography, *Der Tod in Venedig*, ed. T. J. Reed (1971), and in Reed, *Uses of Tradition*. The novella's genesis and its bearing on our understanding and interpretation of the text are discussed in chap. 9.

6. Böhm, *Selbstzucht*, 321. Böhm acutely suggests (323ff.) that Mann's repeated references to the "original" (but really quite different) subject of the old Goethe's (heterosexual) love was "Informationspolitik"; that is to say, a piece of public relations, in fact, virtually "disinformation." A similar view was already implied in the otherwise largely favorable essay on *Death in Venice* by the novelist Wolfgang Koeppen in 1976: "Thomas Mann had a deep-rooted morality of guilt and punishment. He would never willingly put himself among disorderly persons. Tonio Kröger wanted to be like everyone else. A contra-

diction in the artist's existence; Thomas Mann suffered it. . . . 'See things through' [Frederick the Great/Aschenbach's motto "Durchhalten"]—how? By subordinating himself to convention, or by resisting it? For a long time the writer might content himself with his success. The beautiful boy was absorbed into his biography. The disgusting horror-figures of old worn-out, misused, poor homosexuals receded, were replaced by approved [i.e., mythological] figures from the encyclopedia. Passion, the urge of love, is a happiness granted only to the gods. For August von Platen there was death . . . , for Mann-Aschenbach the game with fate, which the more prudent of them won." *Frankfurter Allgemeine Zeitung*, 7 February 1980, excerpted in Bahr, *Erläuterungen*, 163.

7. Myfanwy Piper, *Death in Venice*, an opera in two acts, set to music by Benjamin Britten, opus 88 (London: Faber Music, 1973).

Chapter 4

1. Technically, free indirect style removes the signs which earlier fiction used for distinguishing the character's temporal standpoint from the time frame of the narrative: a verb of thinking or saying in the past tense, followed by direct speech ("She realized: 'This is really happening'"); or by indirect speech ("She realized that this was really happening"), where the character's present tense has become a past tense like that of the main clause by the normal principle of English sequence of tenses. Free indirect style does not thus distinguish narrator's from character's standpoint. It gives us the character's experience in a main clause, but in the narrative past tense ("This was really happening"). With narrator and character drawn thus close together, ambiguity can arise. This is lessened when (as often happens) a fragment of the character's "present-time" experience—typically, an adverb or pronoun—is carried over unchanged into past-tense narration and confirms that we have character, not narrator-viewpoint: "*This* was really happening"; "The water got deeper *here*"; "*Good God*, it could not be done"; "*Now* things were going better." The technique is present systematically as early as Jane Austen in English and Goethe in German. Its most intensive development and subtlest use come with Flaubert in French and with Henry James in English.

For a concise account of the phenomenon and its history, with illuminating examples, see Roy Pascal, *The Dual Voice: Free Indirect Speech and Its Functioning in the Nineteenth-Century European Novel* (Totowa, N.J.: Rowman and Littlefield, 1977).

2. No. 13 in the series *Hundertdrucke* published in Hans von Weber's Hyperion Verlag, Munich. The alternative version of the paragraph in question is reprinted as a variant in my 1983 edition of the German text of *Death in Venice*, 83. (It has also strayed, unaccountably and unexplained, into a recent [1992] reprint of the German text by S. Fischer Verlag.)

3. This does not mean that every detail corresponds to the facts observable on the ground. Divergences like the absence of the "scriptural passages" on the façade, or of obtrusive features in the Venice of 1911, are noted by Krotkoff, "Symbolik," and by Leppmann, "Time and Place."

Chapter 5

1. This function of the story—to serve as an "experiment" in shaping a career and to explore the consequences—means that the "necessities" must have roots in the author's creative world and his problem-filled present. This does not reduce everything to autobiographical statement, since the story goes to dramatic extremes which are pure invention, and achieves general, not merely personal insights. Still, the distinction is a fine one. Readers who are afraid of falling into biographism may prefer to disregard the cross-references between Aschenbach's and Thomas Mann's work in the further notes to this chapter.

2. On "Frederick," "Maya," and "Intellect and Art" as projects of Thomas Mann's, cf. chap. 1, p. 7. On *A Miserable Wretch*, see Hans Wysling, "'Ein Elender': zu einem Novellenplan Thomas Manns," in Scherrer and Wysling (106–22). The transfer of these works to Aschenbach's imaginary oeuvre would have made it difficult for Mann to continue and complete them, so he must have already abandoned the idea by 1912. But he did in 1915 write a long historical essay, "Frederick and the Grand Coalition," and materials from "Intellect and Art" went into (among other works) "Thoughts in War," *Considerations of an Unpolitical Man*, and the 1920s essay "Goethe and Tolstoy." Similarly, many of the themes and figures sketched for "Maya" were used much later in the chapters of *Doctor Faustus* that portray Munich society.

3. A corresponding passage to Aschenbach's "defiant 'Despite'" is Mann's own short essay "Uber den Alkohol" of 1906 (XI, 718). The idea's source is probably Nietzsche's identical statement in *Ecce Homo* ("Zarathustra," sect. 1)—ironically, only one page away from the famous description of the "old-fashioned" inspiration that Nietzsche enjoyed when writing his *Zarathustra*. This was permanently tantalizing for such a laboriously creating modern like Thomas Mann. Cf. *Doctor Faustus*, chap. 25, VI, 316f.

The image of the tense or relaxed hand originated not in any of the literary and philosophical sources from Cicero to Goethe which scholars have conjectured, but in a comment on Hugo von Hofmannsthal made in conversation by the Austrian writer Richard Beer-Hofmann (cf. letter to John Conley, 20 November 1946, *DüD* 1, 443). Hofmannsthal was also the original exemplar of those who "work on the brink of exhaustion" (203). See letter to Heinrich Mann, 7 December 1908.

4. They could not, of course, be named, since—unlike the unfinished projects—they were already publicly Thomas Mann's. Cf. Thomas Mann to

his French translator, Félix Bertaux, 29 March 1924 *DüD* 1, 420f., where he says the figures evoked in his text "resemble," respectively, Thomas Buddenbrook, Lorenzo de' Medici and Savonarola in *Fiorenza*, Prince Klaus Heinrich in *Royal Highness*, and Felix Krull. The phrase used by a "shrewd commentator" to summarize the ethos behind these figures of Aschenbach's (202f.) is the one actually used about Thomas Mann by the critic Samuel Lublinski in his survey of contemporary writing, *Die Bilanz der Moderne* (Berlin: Cronbach, 1904), 226.

5. In Mann's oeuvre, the equivalent work, which captivated a broad popular readership with its "palpably live literary representation," is of course his immensely successful first novel, *Buddenbrooks*.

6. On the literary practice of "insight" and "knowledge," see Tonio Kröger's conversation with Lizaveta Ivanovna (159f.). Significantly, it is already causing that earlier writer-figure extreme discomfort and prickings of conscience.

7. The "ascent to dignity" as an ambition of all artists is alleged by Thomas Mann in "Intellect and Art," n. 59.

8. Cf. again the central dialogue in *Tonio Kröger*. It is expressly the principle "tout comprendre, c'est tout pardonner" that leads Tonio to describe the condition he calls the "nausea of knowledge" (160).

Chapter 6

1. See Thomas Mann to Erika and Klaus Mann, 25 May 1932: "Ambiguous is really the most modest adjective one can give the city (Simmel suggested it)" *DüD* 1, 435.

2. Ernst Bertram, "Das Problem des Verfalls" [1907], reprinted in Bertram, *Dichtung als Zeugnis* (Bonn: Bouvier, 1967).

Chapter 7

1. Mann is not alone in reviving it at this time. Apart from Stefan George's austere circle, there is a striking literary parallel in Rilke's *Duino Elegies*, where love is invoked as the source of a deeper understanding and a spiritual energy that can (and should) carry human beings beyond the beloved. See especially the lines in the First Elegy:

> . . . is it not time that our loving
> made us free from whatever we love, so we tremblingly stand it:
> as the arrow the bowstring, whence gathered for leap-off
> it may be *more* than itself. For of what use is staying?

Plato may have been the source for both writers. Rilke was a friend of Rudolf Kassner, whose versions of *Phaedrus* and the *Symposium* Thomas Mann used, and a letter of Rilke's to Ilse Sadé written at the precisely relevant time and place—5 March 1912 from Castle Duino—shows him reflecting on love in terms avowedly borrowed from Plato's *Symposium*.

Chapter 8

1. By a nice coincidence, the man whose diplomatic travels and persistence established this principle ("the question of international hygiene passes and surpasses political frontiers") was Dr. Adrien Proust, father of the novelist. See George D. Painter, *Marcel Proust: A Biography*, vol. 1 (London: Chatto & Windus, 1961), 2.

2. Mann's knowledge of the Dionysus cult and its rituals came from the scholarly work of Nietzsche's friend Erwin Rohde, *Psyche: Seelencult und Unsterblichkeitsglaube der Griechen*, 4th ed. (Tübingen: J. C. B. Mohr, 1907).

3. The question naturally arises whether Thomas Mann was consciously working in Freudian terms. He tells us that at this stage he had not yet read Freud, but that psychoanalytic theory was "in the air," and that he may conceivably have read things that originated in the Freudian school (letter to Joyce Morgan, 28 February 1951, *DüD* 1, 445f.). Manfred Dierks has suggested ("Schreibhemmung und Freud-Lektüre: Neuer Blick auf die Novelle *Der Tod in Venedig*," *Neue Zürcher Zeitung*, 23–24 June 1990) that the psychological situation and story line of *Death in Venice* follow, and must therefore have been influenced by, Wilhelm Jensen's novel *Gradiva* (1903), as analyzed in an essay of Freud's. But given Mann's disclaimer of a direct Freudian influence, and the fact that the plot follows his situation and experiences of 1911, the hypothesis seems unnecessary. Moreover, the story's psychological theme, the breakup of a controlled life into chaos, was a constant with deep roots in Mann's work (see above, p. 10f.). Dierks had earlier argued in his *Studien* that the story line of *Death in Venice* followed that of Euripides' *Bacchae*. It is not clear how many such determinants a plot line can accommodate.

Chapter 9

1. Gabriele d'Annunzio, *Il fuoco* (1900; reprint, Milan, 1951), 94.

2. The sonnet is the one beginning "Mein Auge liess das hohe Meer zurücke."

3. "Authority on decadence": letter to Malwida von Meysenbug, 18 October 1888; "decadent . . . and its very opposite": in the chapter of *Ecce Homo* entitled "Why I Am So Wise," sect. 2.

4. In this epigrammatic form, the idea comes in a much later work, *Nietzsche contra Wagner*, epilogue, sect. 2.

5. Rohde, *Psyche*, 2:11f.

6. Ibid., 2:42, 47.

7. Friedrich Nietzsche, *Beyond Good and Evil*, sects. 197 and 45. On Nietzsche's beasts of prey as symbols of vitalism in early twentieth-century writing (Mann, Rilke, Benn, Kafka), see my essay "Nietzsche's Animals: Idea, Image and Influence," in *Nietzsche: Imagery and Thought*, ed. Malcolm Pasley (London: Methuen, 1978).

8. To that extent it might have followed out one strand of the short story "A Weary Hour" of the year before. There Mann had decidedly identified with Schiller, among other things with his love-hate for the, to outward appearance, effortlessly creative Goethe. This view is taken to a psychological extreme by Peter von Matt, who suggests that Thomas Mann needed to "kill off" Goethe, the supreme German literary figure, in order to supplant him as *the* "national writer." See "Zur Psychologie des Nationalschriftstellers," in *Perspektiven psychoanalytischer Literaturkritik*, ed. S. Goeppert (Freiburg: Rombach, 1978).

9. The industrialist Alfred Krupp committed suicide in 1902 as a result of journalistic revelations, which were then officially played down. In 1906 Prince Philipp zu Eulenburg, a close friend of Kaiser Wilhelm II, was at the center of similar allegations which led to court proceedings.

10. The word for "song" in this case is *Lied*. But as "*drunken* song," its associations are again high rhapsodic utterance, and specifically the Dionysian elements in Nietzsche: "The Drunken Song" is the title of the last section but one of Nietzsche's *Thus Spake Zarathustra*.

11. The Luke translation of this passage (191) sets "true writer" against "*littérateur*," essence against profession. There is not much more one can do in English to render a distinction which, in bad German criticism, has always appealed to mysticism and snobbery rather than to argument and demonstration.

12. The purely *stylistic* point is put less solemnly in a letter of three weeks later: "I know how difficult it is, when the song [*Lied*] moves in the higher register, not to go over the top into kitsch. In 'D.i.V.' there were tricky passages." Letter to Hans von Hülsen, 22 July 1920, *DüD* 1, 416.

The *social responsibility* point echoes Mann's contribution to Munich debates on art, sex, and society just before and after *Death in Venice*. See Kolbe (158ff.) on Mann and the censoring of Frank Wedekind's plays, and especially the formal opinion Mann gave on the question of literature and public morality in the case of a Munich bookseller who had been attacked for listing erotica in his catalog. (See "Ein Gutachten," in Thomas Mann, *Aufsätze, Reden, Essays*, ed. Harry Matter, vol. 1, *1893–1913* [Berlin: Aufbau, 1983],

220ff.) This statement recognizes that society's demand for sexuality to be "as far as possible hushed up and hidden" is justified, but that art has always disregarded it. Art is "not family entertainment" but a "deep and dangerous thing" that has a "demonic" element rooted in sexuality. This cannot be denied without denying art itself.

At first sight, that is more liberal than the Weber letter because it speaks out for all art, rather than sacrificing a "socially irresponsible" mode (lyric) to save a "socially responsible" mode (narrative). Yet it thereby leaves *all* art in conflict with conservative bourgeois society. The lyric/narrative distinction on the other hand offers a tactical means to infiltrate society by making a taboo subject acceptable. Or is the tactical means merely a surrender? Either way, Thomas Mann was never an "anything goes" liberal. See, just after the Weber letter, his positive but deeply shaken response to the erotic poetry, both homo- and heterosexual, of Verlaine (letter to Paul Steegmann, 18 August 1920). The poems in question are still not included in "complete" works of Verlaine. See Verlaine, *Hombres/Femmes*, dual-text edition, with (virtuoso) translations by Alistair Elliot (London: Anvil Press, 1979).

13. See Hofmiller, "Thomas Mann's *Tod in Venedig*."

14. Georg von Lukács, "Sehnsucht und Form," in the volume of essays *Die Seele und die Formen* (Berlin: Fleischel, 1911).

15. From the letters of 1911–13: *delicacy*: "a very strange subject . . . serious and pure in tone, treating a case of pederasty in an ageing artist. I hear you saying 'hm hm!' But it is all very proper" (to Philipp Witkop, 18 July 1911); *impossible conception*: "tormented by a work which has turned out in the course of execution to be more and more an impossible conception" (to Ernst Bertram, 16 October 1911), "a novella with a daring, perhaps impossible subject" (to Alexander von Bernus, 24 October 1911) [both *DüD* 1, 395], and, "a serious, daring subject. . . . Very important to me to hear from you whether I have made it possible" (to Joseph-Emile Dresch, 21 April 1913, *DüD* 1, 401); *arrangements . . . well advanced* (to Hans von Hülsen, 4 April 1912, *DüD* 1, 396); "still stuck for an ending" (to Heinrich Mann, 27 April 1912); *desperately concerned* (to Albert Ehrenstein, 3 May 1912); *did not know what to think* (to Ernst Bertram, 21 October 1912).

16. On "classical" qualities, see above, p. 13f.; on "mimicry," cf. above, p. 12f., 17.

17. See Cohn, "Second Author." Professor Cohn is tolerant enough of my genetic aproach to say (139) that it only "appears to differ radically" from her intratextual method and is close to it in spirit. So close, one might say, that the "two authors" hypothesis, as she deploys it, is ultimately a metaphor for the real emotional and moral conflict I traced in the writing of the work. Her method may indeed be "a necessary interpretive move for a reader bent on affirming the aesthetic integrity of Mann's novella"—though it is not clear why

we should be "*bent on* affirming" anything that the work of art does not present so persuasively that ingenious hypothesis is not needed to explain discontinuities. At all events, by showing up the real stresses that caused the discontinuities, the genetic approach offers an answer to a textual question—admittedly at the price of emphasizing that the literary work has its roots in (to use a word unfashionable in literary theory) life.

18. Two critics—Vaget, *Kommentar* (199), and Luke, introduction, xli—reject critical accounts that "postulate a 'hymnic origin'" or "postulate a change of course." This is neither frank nor fair. "Postulate" insinuates the critic is offering a speculative hypothesis of his own. But the "hymnic character and origin" ("the *so-called* hymnic origin," says Vaget for good measure [200]) and the "change of course" are Thomas Mann's own unambiguous—confessional, rueful—statements. They are clearer and more fundamental genetic evidence than is commonly found in literary studies, and a conscientious scholar cannot properly neglect them. Luke grudgingly concedes (xlii) that "there *may* have been some shift of emphasis (as *seems to be suggested* by the last two lines of the passage from *Song of the Child*)." When one recalls what those lines actually say:

> There began a process of sobering, cooling, and mastering—
> Lo! what came of your drunken song was an ethical fable

it becomes clear how extraordinary is Luke's refusal to allow words their meaning. Nobody claims that we can (in Luke's phrase) "reconstruct *with certainty* the process of the story's composition," nor that we "*need*" any other version of the story. But that must not be an embargo on attempts to understand, for reasons given in my text, what was obviously an intricate and intense process. And it certainly cannot be a license for reasserting, as Luke does, flatly against the clear sense of Mann's own testimony, that "it is *more likely* that a complexity of conflicting elements was fully present from the beginning" (xlii, all italics mine).

19. Cf. Mann's text p. 234; and of the preparatory note with that passage (work note no. 18), where the Platonic formulations are given as in Plato's text, without any interpolated moral reservations. Is that only because the note contains preparatory, not yet fully processed material? Or do text and note stand on different sides of a genetic divide? Mann later claimed (letter to Paul Amann, 10 September 1915, *DüD* 1, 416)) that the "Greek cultural material" (*Bildungs-Griechentum*) was only a "spiritual refuge of the experiencing subject." Even this statement is ambiguous: does it refer to the "experiencing subject" within the story? Or to the one that had the experiences from which the story originated?

20. Goethe, *Faust*, pt. 1, l. 1112.

Chapter 10

1. In various essays of the mid-1940s. The relevant passages are usefully excerpted in Bahr, *Dokumente*, 165ff. Lukács gets closest when he speaks of *Death in Venice* and Heinrich Mann's *Professor Unrat* as "great harbingers of that tendency which signalled a barbaric underworld within modern German civilisation as its necessary complementary product" (167). Thomas Mann singles out this passage for quotation in his book *The Genesis of Doctor Faustus* (XI, 239).

2. Thomas Mann Archive, Zürich, ms. 33, fol. 8 and 9.

3. Heinrich Mann, "Zola," in the essay volume *Geist und Tat* (reprint, Munich: dtv, 1963), 210. Thomas Mann himself came strangely close to such a recognition. As early as October, he says that reading war propaganda makes you "as savage as if you were in the trenches," speaks of war as "the great blood-drunkenness" (*der grosse Blutrausch*), and suggests that "after the moral orderliness [*Sittsamkeit*] of half a century people are thirsting for horrors,—the whole thing can hardly be explained any other way." He even calls his forthcoming "Thoughts in War" "unspeakably journalistic, a product of corruption" (letter to Annette Kolb, 28 October 1914). The "overcoming" of these insights so that it was still possible to publish the article is itself surely a form of "complicated naiveté."

4. See *Genealogy of Morals*, pt. 1, sect. 11; on barbarians, see the "Nachlass" note in Nietzsche, *Werke*, vol. 3, ed. Karl Schlechta (Munich: Hanser, 1962), 90.

5. *Freud: Standard Edition*, trans. James Strachey, vol. 20 (London: Hogarth Press, 1959), 72.

6. Lawrence, *Selection*, (see n. 1 to ch. 2) 120.

Bibliography

Primary Works

Fiction

Gesammelte Werke. 13 vols. Frankfurt am Main: S. Fischer, 1974. The standard collected, though not complete, edition.

English translations of *Buddenbrooks, The Magic Mountain, Joseph and His Brethren, Doctor Faustus,* and other works by Thomas Mann mentioned in the text are published by Alfred A. Knopf (New York) and by Secker and Warburg (London) in translations by Helen Lowe-Porter. Many of these texts are available as Penguin paperbacks. Alfred A. Knopf has recently launched a retranslation program, beginning with a version of *Buddenbrooks* by John E. Woods (1993).

Death in Venice and Other Stories. Translated with an introduction by David Luke. New York: Bantam Books, 1988.

Der Tod in Venedig. Edited with an introduction and notes by T. J. Reed. Oxford: Clarendon Press, 1971 (and reprints).

Der Tod in Venedig: Text, Materialien, Kommentar. Edited by T. J. Reed. Munich: Hanser, 1983. Contains a complete annotated transcript of Mann's work notes for the story (reprinted in Bahr, *Erläuterungen*). Interested readers are referred to the notes in these critical editions of the German text of *Death in Venice*, which trace Mann's quotations and sources in more detail than it is the job of the present volume to do.

Letters, Diaries, Notebooks

For full details of the original German editions of Mann's diaries and the numerous volumes of correspondence, see *Thomas-Mann-Handbuch*, edited by Helmut Koopmann (Stuttgart: Kröner, 1990), xvif.

The Letters of Thomas Mann. 2 vols. Selected and translated by Richard and Clara Winston. London: Secker and Warburg, 1970.

Diaries 1918–1939. Translated by Richard and Clara Winston. London: André Deutsch, 1983.

Notizbücher 1–6. Edited by Hans Wysling and Yvonne Schmidlin. Frankfurt am Main: S. Fischer, 1991.

Notizbücher 7–14. Edited by Hans Wysling and Yvonne Schmidlin. Frankfurt am Main: S. Fischer, 1992.

Dichter über ihre Dichtungen. Edited by Hans Wysling. Munich: Heimeran, 1975–82. A three-volume collection of Mann's statements about his work, drawn largely from letters, some of them not previously published. Those on *Death in Venice* are contained in vol. 1, 393–448.

"Geist und Kunst" [the notes for the project "Intellect and Art"]. In Scherrer and Wysling, *Quellenkritische Studien.* No English translation exists at present.

Thomas Mann's Main Sources for Death in Venice

Burckhardt, Jacob. *Griechische Kulturgeschichte.* 4 vols. Stuttgart: Kröner, 1898.

*Lukács, Georg von. *Die Seele und die Formen.* Berlin: Fleischel, 1911.

*Plato. *Das Gastmahl* [*Symposium*]. Translated into German by Rudolf Kassner. Leipzig: Diederichs, 1903.

Plato. *Phaidros.* Translated into German by Rudolf Kassner. Leipzig: Diederichs, 1904.

Plutarch. *Erotikos* [*On Love*]. In Plutarch, *Vermischte Schriften.* Leipzig: Müller, 1911.

*Rohde, Erwin. *Psyche: Seelencult und Unsterblichkeitsglaube der Griechen,* 4th ed. 2 vols. Tübingen: Mohr, 1907.

*Thomas Mann's own copy, with his annotations, is preserved in the Zürich Thomas Mann Archive.

Translations of Plato's *Symposium* and *Phaedrus* dialogues can be found in Penguin Classics, in the four-volume Jowett edition (Oxford University Press), and in the one-volume *Collected Dialogues,* edited by Edith Hamilton and

Huntington Cairns, Bollingen Series 71 (Princeton University Press, 1961, and frequent reprints).

Plutarch's dialogue *Erotikos*, translated by W. C. Helmbold, is in vol. 9 of the *Moralia* in the Loeb bilingual edition (Cambridge, Mass.: Harvard University Press, 1969).

Nietzsche's *Birth of Tragedy*, the most important of his works for *Death in Venice*, is available in Penguin Classics, translated by R. J. Hollingdale, and in a version by Walter Kaufman (New York: Random House, 1967).

Biography

Bürgin, Hans, and Hans-Otto Mayer. *Thomas Mann: A Chronicle of His Life.* University of Alabama Press, 1969. The bald facts of Mann's life usefully given in calendar sequence.

Hamilton, Nigel. *The Brothers Mann: The Lives of Heinrich and Thomas Mann.* London: Secker and Warburg, 1978. A readable and well-informed biography of the two men and their uneasy relationship.

Kolbe, Jürgen. *Heller Zauber: Thomas Mann in München 1894–1933.* Berlin: Siedler, 1987. The liveliest biographical work on Mann to date. A well-written and well-documented account—with many atmospheric period photographs—of the Munich background to Mann's (and Aschenbach's) life.

Mendelssohn, Peter de. *Der Zauberer: Das Leben des deutschen Schriftstellers Thomas Mann. Erster Teil 1875–1918.* Frankfurt am Main: S. Fischer, 1975. The first part of what was to be the "official" biography, left unfinished at the death of its author. Already immensely long (1185 pages) because so leisurely in style and so devoted to the detailed narration of unimportant things, it yet manages to leave out much that is essential—for our purposes, the whole issue of Mann's homosexuality and its bearing on *Death in Venice*. The Paul Ehrenberg relationship, too central to be missed, is treated with coy evasiveness. A slighter second volume, edited by Albert von Tschirnding (Frankfurt am Main: S. Fischer, 1993), is subtitled *Jahre der Schwebe 1919 und 1933* and contains two further chapters.

Winston, Richard. *Thomas Mann: The Making of an Artist 1875–1911.* London: Constable, 1982. Likewise unfinished through the death of its author. Broaches the issues de Mendelssohn avoided but finally trivializes them: Mann "perhaps exaggerated" his own homosexual feelings, "as he exaggerated all the little ailments . . . he recorded in his diary" (273).

Secondary Works

A useful list of German and English items, more substantial than there is space for here, is provided in Ehrhard Bahr, *Erl äuterungen und Dokumente zu Thomas Mann "Der Tod in Venedig"* (Stuttgart: Reclam, 1991), 181–95.

Alberts, Wilhelm. *Thomas Mann und sein Beruf.* Leipzig: Xenien-Verlag, 1913. The first monograph on Mann's work to that date, with a stop-press chapter on the newest work, *Death in Venice*, that illustrates contemporary attitudes.

Böhm, Karl Werner. *Zwischen Selbstsucht und Verlangen: Thomas Mann und das Stigma Homosexualität.* Würzburg: Königshausen und Neumann, 1991. Part of a new criticism which appraises Mann's homosexuality and its effects frankly and sympathetically (see also Härle). Polemical towards earlier writers' evasiveness in the face of the evidence. A necessary corrective, though it risks reducing Mann's inspiration and problems to a single source.

Cohn, Dorrit. *Transparent Minds: Narrative Modes for Presenting Consciousness in Fiction.* Princeton, N.J.: Princeton University Press, 1978.

———. "The Second Author of *Der Tod in Venedig*." In *Critical Essays on Thomas Mann,* edited by Inta M. Ezergailis (Boston: G. K. Hall, 1988), 124–43.

Acute work on the techniques of psychological analysis used in modern fiction.

Dierks, Manfred. *Studien zu Mythos und Psychologie bei Thomas Mann.* Berne and Munich: Francke, 1972. Strongly psychoanalytic approach combined with keen pursuit of sources.

Good, Graham. "The Death of Language in *Death in Venice*." *Mosaic* 5, no. 3 (1972): 43–52. Concentrates on the role and implications of silence in the story.

Härle, Gerhard. *Männerweiblichkeit: Zur Homosexualität bei Klaus und Thomas Mann.* Frankfurt am Main: Athenäum, 1988. Similar to Böhm, but with a more psychoanalytic approach. Interpretation is sometimes pressed beyond plausibility to make a case.

Heller, Erich. *The Ironic German.* London: Secker and Warburg, 1957. The first attempt at a synoptic view to be produced after Mann's death in 1955. Still a lively read.

Hofmiller, Joseph. "Thomas Manns *Tod in Venedig*." *Merkur* 9 (1955): 505–20. Reprint of a 1913 article which already spotted essentials about the story's form.

Krotkoff, Herta. "Zur Symbolik in Thomas Manns *Tod in Venedig*." *Modern Language Notes* 82 (1967): 445–53. Compares Munich realities with Mann's realism (see also Leppmann).

Leibrich, Louis. *Thomas Mann: Une recherche spirituelle.* Paris: Aubier, 1975. A comprehensive but concise study by the most prominent French Thomas Mann scholar.

Leppmann, Wolfgang. "Time and Place in *Death in Venice.*" *German Quarterly* 48 (1975): 66–75. Does for Venice 1911 what Krotkoff does for Munich.

Lukács, Georg. *Essays on Thomas Mann.* Translated by Stanley Mitchell. London: Merlin Press, 1964. Fruits of his lifelong sympathetic interest in Mann's work which, where necessary, was stronger than his Marxist axioms.

Reed, T. J. *Thomas Mann: The Uses of Tradition.* Oxford: Clarendon Press, 1974. Interprets Mann's works singly and collectively as a response to and use of German literary, intellectual, and political traditions.

———. "'Geist und Kunst': Thomas Mann's Abandoned Essay on Literature." *Oxford German Studies* 1 (1966): 53–101. Reconstructs the lines of argument of Mann's "Intellect and Art" project and analyzes the conflict of elements that prevented him from completing it.

Scherrer, Paul, and Hans Wysling. *Quellenkritische Studien zum Werke Thomas Manns.* Berne and Munich: Francke, 1967. Masterly genetic and source studies—from the first two curators of the Zürich Thomas Mann Archive—of completed and uncompleted works by Mann, casting much light on his preoccupations and compositional methods. The collection includes the full annotated German text of the notes for "Geist und Kunst" ("Intellect and Art").

Schmidt, Ernst A. "'Platonismus' und 'Heidentum' in Thomas Manns *Tod in Venedig.*" *Antike und Abendland* 20 (1974): 151–78.

———. "'Künstler und Knabenliebe': Eine vergleichende Skizze zu Thomas Manns *Tod in Venedig* und zu Vergils zweiter Ekloge." *Euphorion* 68 (1974): 437–46. Two studies by a classicist of the novella's classical sources and affinities.

Seidlin, Oskar. "Stiluntersuchungen an einem Thomas-Mann-Satz." In Seidlin, *Von Goethe zu Thomas Mann* (Göttingen: Vandenhoeck & Ruprecht, 1963), 148–61. The style analyst's approach to a sentence which can also be treated illuminatingly by the positivist scholar (see Wysling, "Aschenbachs Werke").

Vaget, Hans Rudolf. *Thomas Mann-Kommentar zu sämtlichen Erzählungen.* Munich: Winkler, 1984. A concise treatment of all Mann's shorter fiction, with accounts of its reception and an extensive discussion of secondary works.

Wysling, Hans. "Aschenbachs Werke: Archivalische Untersuchungen an einem Thomas-Mann-Satz." *Euphorion* 59 (1965): 272–314. The alternative approach to Seidlin's.

Other Works

Dodds, E. R. *The Greeks and the Irrational*. Berkeley: University of California Press, 1971. Authoritative study of the earliest documented forms of irrational beliefs.

Dover, K. J. *Greek Homosexuality*. London: Duckworth, 1978. Detailed and dispassionate study of homosexual practices and attitudes to them among the Greeks.

Mitchell, Donald, ed. *Benjamin Britten: Death in Venice*. Cambridge Opera Handbooks. Cambridge: Cambridge University Press, 1987. A collection of essays on various aspects of the opera—its genesis, music, production, and relation to the novella and to the film.

Schmidgall, Gary. *Literature as Opera*. New York: Oxford University Press, 1977. Has an excellent and wide-ranging chapter on Britten's opera which shows equally good judgment on the essentials of the novella.

Index

abyss, 36, 67, 70, 96
adaptations, 18–21
aesthetics, 35, 52, 55, 66
alien, 28, 42–43, 62
"alien god," 10, 28, 59–71
allegory, 32, 95
anagnorisis. *See* recognition
analysis, 6, 36–39, 50, 57, 84, 96
animal imagery, 79
anti-intellectualism, 92–93, 96
Apollo, apolline, 11, 20, 76, 77, 80, 85, 95
archetypes, 11, 78
Aristotle, 59, 69
art, visual, 4, 19, 68
artist story, 10, 91, 102
avantgarde, 6
Aschenbach: "achievement, moralist of," 4, 33, 35, 47, 51, 67, 74; aesthetic, 39, 46, 52, 75; career, 33–40; compositional process, 35, 52–53, 56, 95; "decision" to change direction, 33, 36, 53, 69; death, 71; evo-

lution, 34; family life, 39; final recognition (anagnorisis), 70; happiness, 48–49, 51–52; initial vision, 27–32; love, confession of, 58–59; maturity, 33–34, 53; "master"-status, 25–26, 33–34, 67, 71; parentage, 34; "reborn naiveté," 38; typical characters, 26–27; *von* title, 39; will, 48–49; works, 33–35, 36
Austen, Jane, 115

barbarism, 100–101
beauty, 5, 38–39, 43, 46, 47, 53–55, 58, 60, 62, 67, 80; of surface, 37, 50, 66
Beer-Hoffmann, Richard, 116
Benn, Gottfried, 119
Bertram, Ernst, 114
Bismarck, Otto, Prince von, 3
Blaue Reiter, der, 113
block, writer's, 26–27, 56, 83
Bogarde, Dirk, 19

Bourget, Paul, 4
Britten, Benjamin, 20
Broch, Hermann, 10
Busse, Carl, 16

casual/causal, 48
catastrophe, German, 11, 92, 94,
    100
Catholicism, 16
Chamisso, Adelbert von, 7
cholera, 11, 60–61, 63, 75, 79
civilization, 46, 60, 64, 94, 97
classical, classicism, classicity, 17,
    37–38, 46, 68, 89
compassion, 36, 69
contrary suggestion, code of, 45, 46,
    48, 49, 53, 68
cosmetics, 42–43, 66–67
Crabbe, George, 20
crystal, 8, 72, 73, 89

Dämon, 62
D'Annunzio, Gabriele, 75
Davos, 47
decadence, 5, 75–76
decline, 4–5, 45, 76
description: of Tadzio, 51–52; of
    Venice, 13, 60
destiny, 41–50, 92. See also fate
Dichter16, 84–85
Dickinson, Emily, 8
dignity, of artist, 36, 42, 62, 67, 80,
    87
Dionysus, dionysian, 11, 19, 20, 65,
    76–79, 80, 82, 85, 87, 95, 97,
    100, 101, 118
dream-orgy, 65–67
Dreyfus case, 98

Ehrenberg, Paul, 81
element, unstable (water), 42, 60
emotion as literary fuel, 26
epiphanies, 30–32
erlebte Rede. See style, free indirect

Ernestus, Jørgen, 18
Eros, 10, 56, 70
expansion, dionysian, 30
experiment, Death in Venice as, 8,
    89, 96
explicitness, 39
Expressionism, 17
Eulenburg, Prince Philipp zu, 119
Euripides: Bacchae, 65, 118

fable, moral, Death in Venice as, 12,
    16, 84–86, 90,
façade-explanations. See contrary
    suggestion
failure, Death in Venice as, 84
fascism, 11, 93, 95, 99, 100–101.
    See also Nazism
fate, 10, 11, 41, 43, 49, 62, 64. See
    also destiny
Flaubert, Gustave, 4, 16, 115
forgiveness. See understanding
form, 38, 55; Forms, platonic, 54,
    87
Frederick the Great, 7–8, 35
Freud, Sigmund, 76, 101, 118

genetic approach, 56, 88–90, 121
George, Stefan, 15, 117
Gide, André, 12, 81
Goethe, Johann Wolfgang von, 7,
    16, 80, 89, 115, 119
Goncourt, Edmond, and Jules, 4
Greek, Greeks, 16, 45, 51, 55, 57,
    65, 76, 78, 82

hand-symbolism, 49
Hauptmann, Gerhart, 4, 6
health, as cultural value, 6, 76
Hermes, 11, 79, 86
Hesse, Hermann, 10
hexameter, 46, 86
Hiller, Kurt, 15
Hitler, Adolf, 93, 94, 101
Homer, 46, 51

homosexuality, 12, 15–16, 17–18, 19, 21, 55, 57–59, 75, 80–82, 85
"hymnic origin," "hymnic core," of *Death in Venice*, 84–86, 89, 121

Ibsen, Henrik, 4, 6
Ideas, platonic. *See* Forms, platonic
idyll, 51–58, 60
intoxication, 57, 62, 70, 72, 76, 84, 95, 100
irony, 36, 52, 61; dramatic, 59
irrationalism, 16, 94, 96, 99, 100
isolationism, 93

James, Henry, 10, 20, 115
Jensen, Wilhelm, 118
journey motif, 82–83
Joyce, James, 10
Jung, Carl Gustav, 101
jungle symbol, 28, 64, 78–79

Kafka, Franz, 8, 10, 31, 119
Kandinsky, Wassily, 113
Kant, Immanuel, 52
Kassner, Rudolf, 118
Kerényi, Karl, 100
Kerr, Alfred, 16, 18
Klages, Ludwig, 99
Klee, Paul, 113
knowledge: (*Erkenntnis*), 36–38, 57, 64, 70, 80
Koeppen, Wolfgang, 114
Kronberger, Maximilian, 15

Lawrence, D. H., 12, 16, 100
laxity, moral, 36, 69. *See also* understanding
leitmotiv, 44, 62–63. *See also* recurrence
Lenbach, Franz von, 113
Levetzow, Ulrike von, 80
lie, art as a, 68

"life," as value, 6, 16, 84, 97
literature: moral status of 4; analytic quality of 4; German hostility to, 5; as social criticism, 5; as "spirit," 6; and society, 81
Louis XIV, 38
Lublinski, Samuel, 117
Lukács, Georg (von), 87, 92

Mahler, Gustav, 19–20, 88, 110
mania, 60, 62
Mann, Heinrich (brother), 4, 7, 74, 75, 97, 98, 116
Mann, Katia (wife), 74
Mann, Thomas: ambitions to be a "master," 7; American exile, 11, 92–93; artist-stories, 10; compositional process, 8–9, 73, 83–89, 116; homosexual orientation, 15, 17, 85; intellectuality 88–89; irrationalism confessed, 102; marriage, 7; political opposition to Nazism, 93; puritanism, 86; self-discovery through writing, 9–10; sense of complicity in German history, 96; temptation to change literary mode, 6–7; uncompleted projects, 7, 96, 116; underlying pattern in works, 10–11; vacation in Venice, 8, 74–75

WORKS
Brother Hitler, 94
Buddenbrooks, 3, 5–7, 16, 32, 76, 117
Considerations of an Unpolitical Man, 97, 98, 116
Doctor Faustus, 11, 20, 81, 94, 95, 102, 116
Fiorenza, 7, 89, 93, 117
Frederick and the Great Coalition, 116

The Genesis of Doctor Faustus, 122
German Address: an Appeal to Reason, 100
Germany and the Germans, 94
Gladius Dei, 5, 89
Goethe and Tolstoy, 116
Intellect and Art, 5, 6, 84, 96, 97, 116, 117
Joseph and his Brethren, 10
Little Herr Friedemann, 10
The Magic Mountain, 32, 47, 81
Mario and the Magician, 101
Memoirs of the Confidence Trickster Felix Krull, 81, 83
Royal Highness, 7, 89, 93, 117
A Sketch of my Life, 73
Song of the Child, 83–85, 86
Tonio Kröger, 6–7, 12, 16, 37, 39, 81–82, 84, 89, 91, 96, 97, 117
Thoughts in War, 97, 116, 122
Tristan, 7, 39
Macke, August, 113
Marc, Franz, 113
master, mastery, 7, 10, 13, 17, 25–26, 37–38, 66–68, 71, 88, 92
Maupassant, Guy de, 4
Melville, Herman, 20
metaphysics, 54
Meyer, Agnes, 93–94
mimicry, 12, 17, 89
moralizing, 69
morality, 15, 36–37, 38–39, 55, 58, 61, 64, 68, 86, 89, 91, 94
music, 19, 77, 94–95
myth, 11, 47, 57, 63, 65, 71, 78, 95

narrator, 20, 57
Naturalism, 4–5, 44, 79, 86
Nietzsche, Friedrich, 4, 16, 52, 75, 76–79, 85, 99, 100, 119
Nazism, 92, 102

omens, 25–32, 40, 78, 92
omniscient narrator, 48
orgy, 65–66, 78, 101
outsider, 6, 7, 44
Owen, Wilfred, 20

pathology, 5, 86, 95
pattern, as meaning, 44, 73
Pears, Peter, 19
pederasty, 18, 97
Piper, Myfanwy, 115
"plastic" representation, 6, 13, 36, 51–52. *See also* description
Platen, August von, 75
Plato, 54–58, 67–68, 82, 87, 89
plausibility, 30. *See also* realism
plot-line, 47, 59
Plutarch, 82
politics, 5, 92, 94, 97–100
Proust, Adrien, 118
Proust, Marcel, 12
Prussianism, 34, 92
psychology, 11, 50, 57, 62, 76–79, 82, 89, 100

rationality, 27, 62, 98
Realism, 11, 28, 30–31, 63–64, 71, 79, 95
reality, behind appearances, 45, 48; transcendent. *See* Forms, platonic
recognition, 49, 54, 59, 68, 70
recurrence, of characters, 32–44, 62. *See also* leitmotiv
regeneration, 6, 76, 82–83, 95–96
rejuvenation, 43, 66
relativism, 34
Rembrandt, 113
Rilke, Rainer Maria, 10, 117–119
Rousseau, Henri ("Douanier"), 113

Saint Sebastian, 19
satire, 5
satyr-play, 47

Index

Schiller, Friedrich, 35, 119
Schopenhauer, Arthur, 32
Schriftsteller, 84
science, 5
sea, as ideal, 46; as refuge, 87
self-simplification, 38, 94
Shakespeare, 20
Simmel, Georg, 43
skepticism, 13–14, 36, 39
sobriety, 53, 62, 64, 84
Socrates, 46, 54, 66, 68, 87
song, 83–84, 119
society, 5, 81, 85, 88–89, 95, 99
sordidness, 42–43, 60
Sorel, Georges, 99
spirit, 6, 47, 55, 57, 67
Staël, Madame de, 36
Stendhal, 52
Stuck, Franz von, 113
style, 10, 12–13, 15–17, 25–26, 68;
    free indirect (narrative
    mode), 27–29, 48, 52,
    115
symbolism, 32, 44–45, 54, 75, 84

taboo, 17, 85
thesis, 44
theater, 30, 42
Tolstoy, Lev Nikolaevich, 4
tragedy, 36, 59, 69, 76, 87, 92, 96,
    101
Turgenev, Ivan Sergeyevich, 4

understanding, 36–37, 69–70

Van Gogh, Vincent, 113
Venice: as a city of decadence, 75;
    composition begun in, 13, 84;
    cultural associations of 74–75;
    description of, 13, 60; effect
    of climate, 47; as real setting,
    31–32; as tourist trap, 60;
    Mann's vacation in, 8, 74–75
Verlaine, Paul, 120
Versailles treaty, 99
verse, 83, 85–86
Vienna, 101
vitalism, 79

Wagner, Richard, 75–77
Wall Street crash, 99
Weber, Carl Maria, 85–87
Weber, Hans von, 115
Wedekind, Frank, 11
Weimar Republic, 99
Wilde, Oscar, 18, 82
Wilhelm II, kaiser, 5, 119
World War I, 91–92, 97–99
World War II, 93–94

Xenophon, 46

youth, as cultural value, 36, 43

Zola, Emile, 5, 98

The Author

T. J. Reed is Taylor Professor of German Language and Literature at the University of Oxford, and a Fellow of the Queen's College. He was born in Blackheath, London, in 1937, went to a London grammar school, and took his degree in modern languages at Brasenose College, Oxford, in 1960. He has taught at Oxford for over 30 years, 25 of them as Fellow and Tutor in German at St. John's College. His publications include *Thomas Mann: The Uses of Tradition* (1974); *The Classical Centre: Goethe and Weimar 1775–1832* (1980); *Goethe* (1984); *Schiller* (1991); critical editions of Thomas Mann's *Der Tod in Venedig*, for both English (1971) and German readers (1983); a verse translation of Heine's satirical poem *Germany, A Winter's Tale* (1986); and numerous articles on German literature and ideas from the mideighteenth century to the 1990s. He co-edits the yearbook *Oxford German Studies* and is editor of the *Oxford Magazine*, the university's house journal. He was elected a Fellow of the British Academy in 1987. He is married, with two children. Outside the family, he is happiest when teaching or mountain walking.

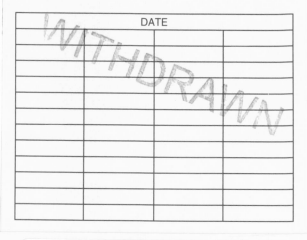